Changes for Technical Education

Chandan T. Bhunia

ATLANTIC
PUBLISHERS & DISTRIBUTORS (P) LTD

Published by

ATLANTIC

PUBLISHERS & DISTRIBUTORS (P) LTD

B-2, Vishal Enclave, Opp. Rajouri Garden,
New Delhi-110027
Phones : +91-11-25413460, 25429987, 25466842

Sales Office
7/22, Ansari Road, Darya Ganj,
New Delhi-110002
Phones : +91-11-23273880, 23275880, 23280451
Fax : +91-11-23285873
web : www.atlanticbooks.com
e-mail : info@atlanticbooks.com

Branch Office
5, Nallathambi Street, Wallajah Road,
Chennai-600002
Phones : +91-44-64611085, 32413319
e-mail : chennai@atlanticbooks.com

Printed in India
at Nice Printing Press, Delhi

Preface

I firmly believe that the developing or poor nations can compete with the developed countries only by means of generating more and improved human resources. To achieve this, I believe, the system and the structure and the policies and the programme of higher education in the developing countries need to be made cost-effective, productive and qualitative. In order to achieve a better form of higher education system, structure, policies and programmes for the developing nations, I had an immense urge to do some research on personal capacity. Accordingly, I carried out research and conducted a few surveys based on which I published several papers in the journals/conferences/newspapers, a few of which are: "Institute-Cum-Industry", *J. University News*, Association of Indian Universities (August 1994); "Person-Power Development: Why and How," *CSI Communication*, Computer Society of India (March 1996); "Technical Education and Training for the Information Age," *J. Productivity*, Vol. 39, No. 4, (Jan-March 1999); "Information Technology in Human Resources Development," *J. Personnel Today* (Jan-March 1998); "Institute-Cum-Industry Revisited," *J. University News*, Association of Indian Universities (November 1995); "Higher Education Restructuring and Productivity," *J. University News*, Association of Indian Universities (January 2000); "Overcoming

High Expenses of Higher Education," *J. University News*, Association of Indian Universities (June 2003); "Planning for Higher Technical Education in Changed Scenario," *J. University News*, Association of Indian Universities (December 2004); "Hybrid Approaches in Higher Education," *J. University News*, Association of Indian Universities (2004); and "Technical Education: Some Thoughts," *J. University News*, Association of Indian Universities (January 2003).

Later, on inspiration of many friends, I attempted to write a book over the work. Hence is the present exercise. I am grateful to my family members, friends and relatives for giving me inspiration to complete the exercise. Special thanks to Mamoni for taking care of Sweet when I fully kept myself engaged in preparing this work. I am grateful to Niti, Sweet and Sabuj for allowing me and inspiring me to write this book.

I feel honor to dedicate this book to all of my teachers who made me what I am today.

C.T. Bhunia

Introduction

Appropriate Technical Education Systems and Structures and Policies and Programme for the Developing Countries in the Age of IT and LPG

Since the last quarter of the last century, the whole of the world has witnessed a transition to global society, global economy and global village. This is due to wide acceptance of and participation in the process of LPG (Liberalization, Privatization and Globalization) world over. The process of LPG has flourished with the evolution and revolution of information that is solely due to the single most technology known as IT (Information Technology). IT has grown leaps and bounds unparallel to any other technology over any recorded period of history. Many authoritative studies have established the globalization process as a means for development, growth and prospects. At the same time some other equally authoritative studies sighted a different gloomy picture of globalization process and established that the existing gap between the rich and the poor will widen during globalization or open economy. In our study presented here, we have tried to respect both the views, and from the critical analysis of the views we have reported a few means of taking part in the globalization process for the developing countries or poor countries. By these means we believe that the developing countries will be leaders in the globalization process rather than followers. We have established in our studies that more quality and skillful human resources generation will be a sound strategy for the developing nations in taking part in open economy. Our view has been collaborated by studies of many other scientists, thinkers and philosophers. But to generate more and highly qualitative and skill oriented human resources, we need to restructure the systems, the policies and the programs of higher technical education keeping in mind our financial resources' crunch and our environmental and geographical requirements. In our work, we have taken India as one example of developing nations, and most of the analysis presented here has been made in reference to India.

Our work is reported in the following order and sections. As we are living in the age of information technology, it will be most appropriate to analyze our position first and foremost in light of information technology's role in shaping the developing countries. In fact in Section 1 of our studies, we have taken up digital divide as a single most parameter for analyzing and finding solutions for the problems of the developing countries if any after analyzing so. Section 2 deals with the establishment of the lemma that "more and improved, knowledgeable and skillful human generation will be a sound strategy for the developing nations in the age of globalization." Section 3 reports the problem of the developing countries to implement the strategy, vis-à-vis, the problem of state funding for improved and high level human generation. The section provides also a solution to this problem. A solution for the technical education suggested in the work is known as ICI (Institute-Cum-Industry). The extensive analysis on ICI has been given in the section including a case study, result of a survey on ICI, and the comparison of ICI with existing conventional universities in terms of expenditure and productivity. In Section 4 we have reported that in addition to ICI form of the structural modifications of the institute, the structural modification in courses are needed in the developing countries. The structural change in courses has become imperative, as the developing countries need to give some quantum jump to create more and improved human resources on immediate basis in order to compete with the developed countries. The structural changes are also the need of hour in view of the increasingly private participation in technical education that has resulted in exponential increase in enrollment. The increase in enrollment has in turn made possible either non-eligible or near eligible candidates in getting admission in higher technical education. Until and unless structural change is made, the effect of enrollment as told is bound to degrade the quality of outputs of higher technical education. The suggested structural changes in the courses are named as FARE (Fast And Rapid Education) and SARE (Slow And Recurring Education). Recently in the higher education a new trend has been noticed in the developing countries. The new trend is to invite private participation in the higher education and reduction of state funding in the higher education. Without any comment, it will be nice to quote here V.V. Krishnan, Center for Studies in Science Policy, JNU, New Delhi. He told in reference to the decision making that "This should not be monopolized by a scientific and political elite, often joined by private corporate interests." The message is clear, and the new policy decision taken by the developing countries, therefore, hardly is in the most cases not believed to be as not counter-productive. In Section 5, we have critically reviewed the state of private initiatives in the higher education. Our question in this regard: Do we need private investment in technical education or privatized technical education? What exactly are we practicing? We have analyzed the present scenario in light of these. In the section we have studied the dual and contradictory policies of government in implementing the globalization process, and we have shown in certain cases, how the government is following cyclic wrong path. In Section 6, we have reported some measures to maintain quality in the education process. In Section 7, we have given a conclusion in pictorial form, which we understand ICI, FARE & SARE, PAD (Posting, Assessment, Duties and Discipline) and FILL (Faculty, Internet, Library and Laboratory) as described in subsequent sections will be solid and sound guidelines for the developing nations to follow for taking part in the globalization process as leaders rather than followers.

Contents

Analysis and Solutions for Digital Divide for the Developing Nations to Take Part in Competitive Globalized Process

1

With IT in hand, the countries are classified into groups of "Information Rich" and "Information Poor". The classification is based on the figures of access to information and IT tools that includes telecommunication, computer, Internet, wireless and broadband access. It is established that the developed nations belong to information rich category and the developing nations to the information poor category. The division is given a name digital divide (DD). The DD exists in other forms also based on income level, education level, gender, language, etc. This belies the other reports that with IT, the economic growth and development is guaranteed. In the section, both the pictures are analyzed with different figures and reports. The future trends are also examined. The missing link between the two contradictory aspects of digital divide is investigated and possible solutions are suggested. The solutions are aimed towards community informatics, industrial barga and new system of education meant respectively for allowing benefits of IT to reach to rural masses, raising the national per capita income and raising the technical skill oriented education level respectively. These together may offer an integrated solution to problems the technology faces in achieving its main aim to reduce the gap between the "haves" and the "have nots." This is first and foremost for any nation before taking part in globalized competition.

1.1 INTRODUCTION

Scientific research has conclusively established that man is a part of nature. The technology that is an application of science has since thus following the science has now attained to implement animalization of machine and vice versa, the latest manifestation of which is the intelligent computer and its predicted applications. While the aim of science is to find answer to "why nature is like as it is" or "what makes nature as it is"; the technology apparently speaking or as is told, aims to address the central social issues of reducing poverty and the gap between "haves" and "have nots." But critical looks belie the goals of the technology. Neither the poverty has been eliminated on the mother earth nor the gap between the rich and the poor has been reduced in past ages of industrial technology and in the present age of information technology. At present scenario it is widely unexpected to see any reverse trend in the coming up knowledge society, that is supposed to be guided by the weightless economy, knowledge workers and knowledge factories. Before we critically look into the issues, it will be undoubtedly desirable to look into the problem in depth. In the present age of the information technology, the problem of disparity has been given a technical name called "Digital Divide" (DD), that defines the division of the society into parts of those having access to information and those not having. In general all the developed countries belong to "Information Rich" and the rest of the world to "Information Poor." An overview of the facts and figures to understand the gravity of the digital divide may be desirable. The IT amounts to Computer, Networks and Communication. Accordingly, the digital divide will be looked in reference to Internet, PCs, and Telecommunication. In the present age of IT, there is a concerted prediction that the future is with BRIC (Brazil, Russia, India and China). There is a need to investigate how far the BRIC is from its goal and/or how near they are to achieve their goal. At the same time, several reports and investigations have come to some definite judgment, may not be conclusive judgment that IT adds to prosperity both economically and growth wise. Therefore, there is an immediate need to research and investigate the missing link, if any and to suggest remedial measures. The present work aims in that direction. Tagore once said, "we have only one country in this universe, and that is the world." Rabindranath Tagore's powerful philosophy may ultimately realize if today's tenet of "one world one village" is implemented in true sense in future and the mindful processes of applications. To achieve this, a trend has already been initiated the world over: Privatization. Liberalization and Globalization are replacing liberty, fraternity and equality all over the world including the countries of Third World. It does not mean that liberty and fraternity have no relevance in today's society. They are ever alive and their universal appeal shall ever remain for the noble human society, but to-day they are not all in all. Privatization and universalization will be the other social partners with them. This is a wave brought forward by different emerging technologies that are often interactive, interdependent and diffusive. Information technology, computer, communication, micro-electronics, genetic engineering, bio-technology, space technology are a few to name worthy. Developing world in general is far lagging behind the modern technological evolutions and revolutions. Besides, the developing, countries are hardly having capital to deal with such fast, rapid and perpetual changes. Developing world in general is labor intensive rather than capital intensive. Therefore, debate on the ability, the suitability and the acceptability of liberalization is going on and will continue to go on for some more time in the developing countries. Initial mismatch and inertia are parts of life and the fact is that the society never denies mobility. The society ultimately accepts technological changes, which might be off-touch to the society, even a few years back. And irony is that such delayed acceptance is done in quite haphazard and irregular ways. We can sight a figure to justify this. Telecommunication lines of India are 66% digitized, whereas figures of Brazil and Hungary are 35.7% and 41% respectively. But the fault figures are 218 faults per 100 lines in India and 2 faults per 100 lines in USA and Japan. Better is not the sole dimension of competitive advantages; faster is equally another important dimension. Thus, it will be a sound strategy for the developing countries to take part in the globalization without any further loss of time, but with intelligent, selective, judicious and strategic applications of globalization process, with innovative applications of emerging technologies of which Internet and IT are the front runners. But the unmindful application of the technology will be suicidal in nature. With this in mind, a thorough picture of IT in world with different parameters is critically looked into this section before proposing a few innovative solutions. The section deals with facts and figures of DD in reference to the world, the regions and the countries. The selection of the regions and the countries are made in relevance with an the developing countries in general and India & BRIC in particular. The future of DD has been investigated with an empirical formula. This investigation shows that the DD will continue to widen in future. Therefore, immediate mindful application of IT is the need of the hour to stop further erosion. We are of the opinion that the process of application must not be copied from the developed nations. We may share the developed nations' experience but we need to formulate our strategies considering our socio-economic fabric. The section also reports the significant and productive achievements this world has witnessed with IT revolution. The missing link between DD and IT's economic achievement has been analyzed. Based on the analysis and investigation, a few possible solutions have been proposed for the developing countries.

1.2 DD BETWEEN THE DEVELOPED AND THE DEVELOPING COUNTRIES

The International Telecommunication Union (ITU) used an index known as Digital Access Index (DAI) to rank/classify the countries[1]. The DAI was determined by factors like the affordability to Internet access, education, the percentage of high-speed Internet users and the availability of the raw bandwidth. Table (1.1) lists the ranking of countries as per DAI calculated by ITU.

The present scenario in terms of latest Internet Usage data and penetration (% population) of the different world regions[2] is portrayed in Figure 1.1. The same type of mismatch is found in Table 1.1 and in Figure 1.1 between the developed and the developing countries in the world. The wide mismatch both in absolute terms of Internet usage and penetration percentage is found in between the developed and the developing countries. The picture of BRIC is bleak. The percentage penetration of Asia, Africa, Middle East and Latin America is below the world's 11.5%. Only USA, Oceania and Europe are above the world figure of 11.5%. The significant observation is that Oceania beats the Europe. A glimmering disparity is illustrated

Table 1.1: DAI ranking as per ITU

RANK	Country	Remarks
1	Sweden	First twenty countries include: • Most of developed and G-5 countries like USA, UK, Germany, Japan • But prominent missing countries are France, Italy, Russia • A few small but rising countries like South Korea, Hong Kong and Taiwan • A few other small countries like Iceland, Finland, Norway, etc.
2	Denmark	
3	Iceland	
4	South Korea	
5	Norway	
6	Netherlands	
7	Hong Kong	
8	Finland	
9	Taiwan	
10	Canada	
11	USA	
12	UK	
13	Switzerland	
14	Singapore	
15	Japan	
16	Luxembourg	
17	Austria	
18	Germany	
19	Australia	
20	Belgium	
—	—	Most striking issues are: • The developed countries in general belong to top ranking DAI • The developing and poor countries belong to lower ranking DAI • So far people are expecting BRIC (Brazil, Russia, India and China) as the rising sun. But none of these countires is in even first fifty! **Is there any wrong in our prediction?**
63	Russia	
64	Mexico	
65	Brazil	
—	—	
78	South Africa	
—	—	
84	China	
—	—	
119	India	
—	—	
153	Nigeria	
—	—	
174	Guinea Bissau	Last five countries
175	Chad	
176	Mali	
177	Burkina Faso	
178	Niger	

Fig. 1.1(a) **Internet usage on different zones world over operator**

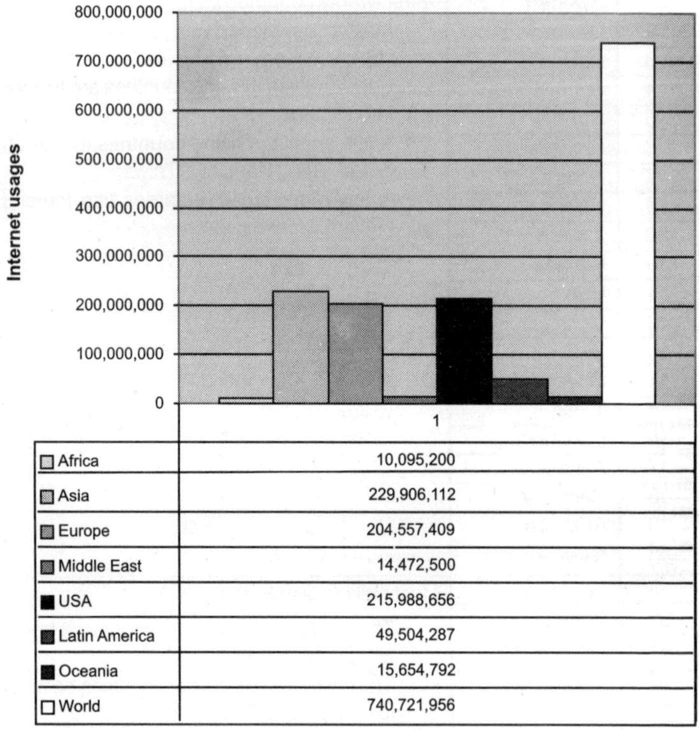

Africa	10,095,200
Asia	229,906,112
Europe	204,557,409
Middle East	14,472,500
USA	215,988,656
Latin America	49,504,287
Oceania	15,654,792
World	740,721,956

in Table (1.2). It is found that the world's only about 20% lucky population living in the developed nations in USA and Europe have about 60% Internet access, and the poor vast population of about 70% mostly living in Asia and Africa have only about 30% world Internet access. A disparity of such a huge volume is surely a cause of concern for the technology, the technologists, and the policy-makers. In Table (1.3), a comparison in terms of plus- minus parameters is made for the top ten countries in the world. The plus axis refers to top ten countries having highest number of Internet users, top ten countries with highest penetration ratio and top ten countries with highest per capita income[3]. The minus axis refers to top ten countries with highest population, along with

Fig. 1.1(b)

Internet penetration world over

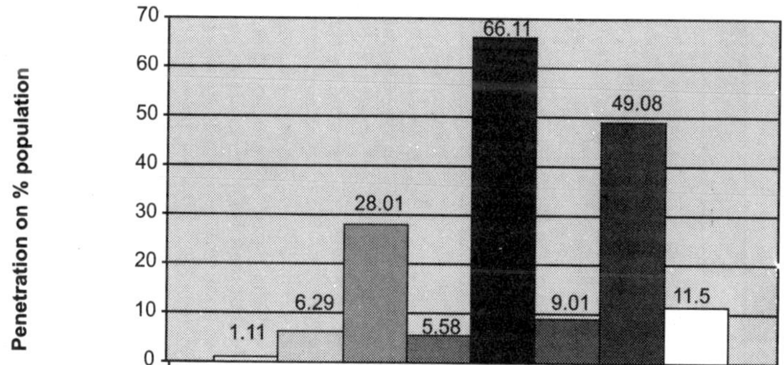

Africa	1.11
Asia	6.29
Europe	28.01
Middle East	5.58
USA	66.11
Latin America	9.01
Oceania	49.08
World	11.5

Fig. 1.1 : Internet usages, Online people and Internet penetration world over (the data are of latest as in March 2004)
[Appendix A may be seen for some recent figures]

Table 1.2: DD over different regions

Country	% of world total Internet usage	% of world total population (Country's population) as estimated for 2004	Remark
Africa	1.36%	14.03% (905954600)	In the world, USA and Europe together have 16.33% of total world population, and 56.67% Internet usage.
Asia	31.03%	56.6% (3654644000)	
Europe	27.61%	11.29% (728857380)	
Middle East	1.95%	4.01% (259166000)	
USA	29.06%	5.06% (326695500)	Asia and Africa together have 70.63% of total world population with a meager 32.39% Internet usage.
Latin America	6.68%	8.46% (546100900)	
Oceania	2.11%	0.49% (31892487)	Such a huge disparity exists in the year 2004

Table 1.3: DD over different countries

Positive Axis				Negative Axis			
Top Ten countries in terms of highest Internet users (in 2004)	Top Ten countries with highest Internet penetration (% population) (in 2004)	Top Ten countries with highest per capita income (in 2002)	Countries with frequency 2 or more in the positive axis	Top ten countries with highest population in the world (in 2004)	The countries with Internet penetration rate (% population) (in 2004) below world average of 11.5% — Yes or No?	The countries with rank below 100 in per capita income (in 2002) — Yes or No?	Countries with frequency 2 or more in the negative axis
USA	Sweden	Bermuda	Frequency 3: USA only	China	Yes (6.5%)	Yes (rank 136)	Frequency 3: China, India, Indonesia, Pakistan, Nigeria, Bangladesh. Frequency 2: Brazil, but if the marginal figures are considered for Brazil and Russia, the Brazil has frequency 3 and Russia 2. almost all world highest populated developing countries fall in the group. no developed country has any place. the picture of bric is gloom.
China	USA	Luxembourg	Frequency 2: Japan, South Korea, Iceland, Denmark, Switzerland in the list, no place is there for any developing country. no place of bric too.	India	Yes (1.5)	Yes (rank 162)	
Japan	Australia	Norway		USA	No (66.11%)	No (rank 6)	
Germany	Netherlands	Switzerland		Indonesia	Yes (3.6%)	Yes (rank 146)	
UK	Hong Kong	Liechtenstein		Brazil	Yes (11.2%)	**No (but rank 96)**	
South Korea	Iceland	USA		Pakistan	Yes (1%)	Yes (rank 168)	
France	Denmark	Japan		Nigeria	Yes (0.35)	Yes (rank 180)	
Brazil	South Korea	Channel Islands		Russia	**No**	**No (but rank 100)**	
Italy	Singapore	Denmark		Bangladesh	Yes (0.1%)	Yes (rank 172)	
Canada	Switzerland	Iceland		Japan	No (44.75)	No (rank 7)	

The weighted mean of frequency for positive axis = (17 X 1 + 5 X 2 + 1 X 3) /23 = 1.3. So fortune countries are those with frequency > 1.3 and these are USA, Japan, South Korea, Iceland, Denmark, Switzerland.

The weighted mean of frequency for negative axis = (3 X 1 + 1 X 2 + 6 X 3) /10 = 2.3. The misfortune countries are with frequency > 2, and these are : India, China, Indonesia, Pakistan, Nigeria and Bangladesh (5 countries of Asia, and 1 country of Africa).

their Internet usage penetration ratio and per capita income. The comparison gives an evidence that the countries with higher per capita income and comparatively (in relation to geographic area, of course the other proper term may be population density) are having higher penetration ratio. The inference columns of the positive axis and the negative axis clearly demonstrate a co-relation between population and per capita income on the one hand with Internet usages and penetration ratio on the other. The gloomy picture of BRIC is further established. However, the evidence of co-relation may be explained by the following: (a) with higher per capita income, the number of Internet users may increase, as with higher income, the affordability of Internet access will increase directly. Again with higher per capita income, education level will increase that will result in indirect increase of Internet users, and (b) the higher population of the developing countries and lower average education level of the countries, results in lower penetration ratio. Table (1.4) portrays the standings of countries in terms of current and future IT tools respectively in form of PCs and Internet access and Mobile users and Broadband technologies. It is found that: (a) Africa, Asia, China, India, Russia and Brazil are below the world average in each case except that the Russia is marginally above the world average in case of telephone lines per 100 inhabitants only; and the Brazil is marginally above the world average in respect to telephone lines and Cellular subscribers per 100 inhabitants. Thus the hope of BRIC is not guaranteed. (b) In the world's topper list, only USA has frequency 2, and the countries with frequency 1 are South Korea, Iceland, Taiwan and Switzerland. (c) One observation of concern is that Europe is below world average in Internet Hosts per 10,000 inhabitants. (d) As expected, the electricity consumption (this is surely determined by the electricity availability) has a direct relation with IT uses and accesses. The picture of BRIC is still gloom in this case too. Except Russia, all other three countries, namely India, China and Brazil are below the world average.

Thus it is established that to minimize DD, the developing countries need to ensure: (a) increased per capita income, (b) education level, and (c) higher level of electric power

Table 1.4: IT of different countries[4]

Electricity Consum-ption per 10,00,000 persons in kWh	Countries	Information Technology (in 2002)			Telephone lines in k (in 2002)	Cellular mobile subscribers (in 2002)	Broadband services (in 2002)
		Internet Hosts per 10,000 inhabitants	Internet users per 10,000 inhabitants	PCs per 100 inhabitants	Telephone lines per 100 inhabitants	Subscribers per 100 inhabitants	Broadband subscribers per 100 inhabitants with world rank in bracket()
	Africa	**3.01**	**123.01**	**1.30**	**2.77**	**4.59**	
	Asia	**37.08**	**584.69**	**4.45**	**11.99**	**12.42**	
0.103	China	1.22	460.09	2.76	16.69	16.09	
0.474	India	0.75	159.14	0.72	3.98	1.22	
5.02	Hong Kong	586.72	4301.14	42.20	56.91	94.25	14.6 (2)
7.58	Japan	726.65	4488.56	38.22	55.83	63.65	6.1 (13)
5.73	South Korea	85.57	5518.91	55.58	48.86	67.95	21.3 (1)
8.10	Singapore	812.60	5043.59	62.20	46.29	79.56	5.5 (14)
6.09	Taiwan	963.66	3814.26	39.46	58.17	106.15	9.4 (4)
	America	**1450.21**	**2575.99**	**28.95**	**34.73**	**29.90**	
12.5	USA	3998.77	5513.77	65.89	64.58	48.81	6.5 (11)
16.01	Canada	953.07	5128.29	48.70	63.55	37.72	11.5 (3)
1.853	Brazil	128.68	822.41	7.48	22.32	20.06	
	Europe	**230.38**	**2169.95**	**21.44**	**41.34**	**51.26**	
6.82	Austria	450.95	4093.64	36.93	48.88	78.62	6.6 (9)
7.56	Belgium	325.04	3283.17	24.14	49.44	78.56	8.4 (7)
	Denmark	1556.74	5128.15	57.68	68.86	83.32	8.6 (6)
	Iceland	2370.17	6479.17	45.14	65.28	90.60	8.6 (5)
6.98	France	232.86	3138.32	34.71	56.89	64.70	
14.65	Finland	2343.12	5089.30	44.17	52.35	86.74	5.3 (15)
6.14	Germany	314.32	4119.38	43.13	65.09	72.75	
6.16	Netherlands	1937.14	5063.29	46.66	61.77	74.47	6.5 (10)
5.37	Russia	27.92	409.32	8.87	24.22	12.01	
7.33	Switzerland	770.34	3510.38	70.87	74.42	78.93	6.3 (12)
15.11	Sweden	949.54	5730.74	62.13	73.57	88.89	7.7 (8)
5.8	UK	485.03	4230.98	40.57	59.06	84.07	
	Oceania	**968.42**	**3698.06**	**42.43**	**40.40**	**84.87**	
9.38	Australia	1304.21	4817.41	56.51	53.86	63.98	
Around 3	**World**	**258.64**	**1022.78**	**9.91**	**17.90**	**19.07**	

OBSERVATIONS

Africa, Asia, China, India, Russia and Brazil are below the world average in each case except the Russia is being marginally above average in case of telephone lines per 100 inhabitants only and the Brazil is being marginally above the telephone lines and cellular subscribers per 100 inhabitants. Thus the hope of BRIC is not guaranteed. The earlier conclusion in respect of BRIC stands well.

In the world's topper lists only the USA has frequency 2, and other countries with frequency 1 are South Korea, Iceland, Taiwan and Switzerland. One observation of concern is that Europe is below world average in Internet Hosts per 10,000 inhabitants. As expected, the electricity consumption (this is surely determined by the electricity availability) has a direct relation with IT uses and accesses. The picture of BRIC is still gloom in this case too. Except Russia, all other three countries, namely India, China and Brazil are below world average.

availability. Comparing the Brazil's way of globalization with that of South Korea's way, Nobel Laureate Prof. Amartya Sen reportedly and repeatedly urged that in the developing countries the social infrastructure like education must be kept under state sponsorship while the physical infrastructure like electricity (power sector) be left to private sector. We are in dilemma till date on implementing the concluding judgment of Prof. Sen.

1.3 DD TREND IN FUTURE

The issue may be highlighted with a single parameter of IT penetration rate over population. It is not the absolute number of Internet, PCs, etc. of a country that will make it "information rich", but the penetration rate over population. The yearly growth of IT access of a country and that of the population of that country determine the penetration rate of IT. Mathematically speaking, the stated relation be given as:

$(dN/dP) = (dN/dY)/(1/ (dP/dY)$ where: dN/dP = penetration rate, dN/dY = growth rate of IT access over years, and dP/dY = population growth with respect to years.

While for the developed countries the reasonable empirical relations between N and Y and between P and Y will be:

$N = a\ Y^2$ and $P = b\ Y$;

those for the developing countries will be at best:

$N = c\ Y^2$ and $P = d\ Y^2$ where a, b, c and d are constants. The reasonableness is based on the Fig. 1.2 that portrays the growth pattern, population and Internet users, for a few selected countries over years.

Thus over the coming years, the penetration rate for the developed and the developing countries will grow at the rate of A, Y and B respectively, where A (= 2aY/b) and B (= c/d) are constants. This amounts to say that in coming years, whereas the growth for developing countries will increase over time, the penetration growth of the developing countries will remain a flat one. This may be called negative avalanche for gap reduction in technology.

Penetration rate of the developed nations ÷ Penetration rate of the developing nations is proportional to years in numbers from any current reference to any future reference

...(1)

Fig. 1.2(a) **Growth Rate of Internet Users**

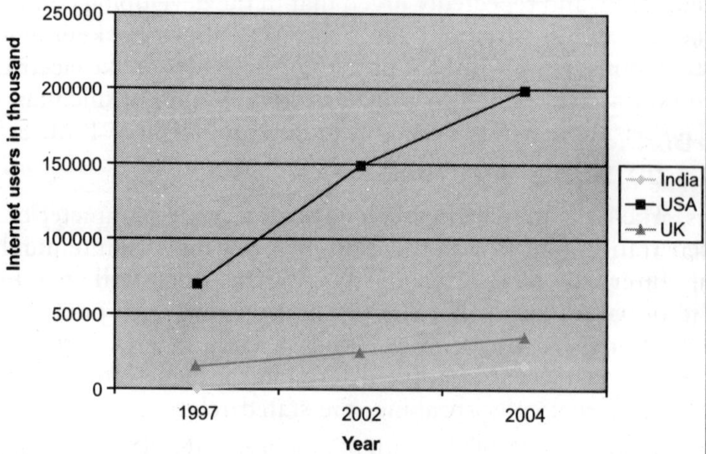

Fig. 1.2(b) **Global Population Growth**

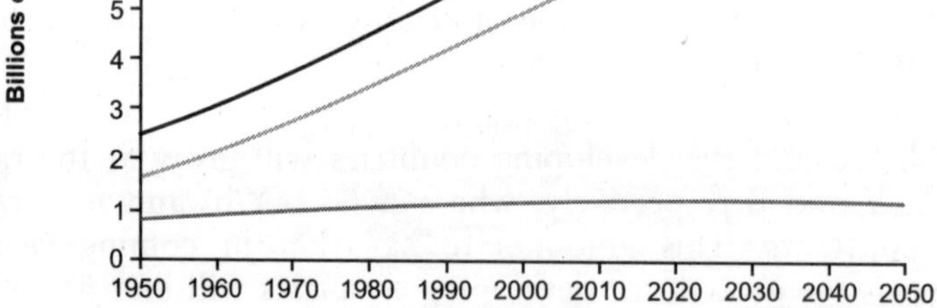

Note: (b) of Fig.1.2 (as per www on environmental Issues) : We find a close relation between our empirical relation and the www on environmental Issues. This justifies our comments based empirical relation

Fig 1.2: Growth pattern for Internet Users and Population[5] for a few selected countries over a few years.

This is due to disparity in growth of the population between the developed and the developing nations. Thus the digital divide will increase over time and as per the model proposed, the gap will grow linearly with time until and unless some drastic, innovative, appropriate and corrective measures are taken.

1.4 DD BETWEEN INDIA AND CHINA

The hope of BRIC is not evident at least and as far as the facts and figures sighted earlier are concerned. In the BRIC, India and China both belong to Asia. It will be therefore proper to investigate DD if any in between these two projected giant countries of Asia. Table (1.5) shows the comparison.

Table 1.5: DD in between China and India

	India	China	Remarks
Population in 2004	1,088,056,200	1,327,976,727	Comparatively same
Internet users in 2000	5,000,000	22,500,000	Wide gap, India lags
Internet users in 2004	16,580,000	79,500,000	Wide gap, India lags
Users' growth over 2000-2004	231.6%	253.3%	Comparatively same
Internet penetration in % (population) 2004	1.5%	6.0%	Wide gap, India lags
PCs per 100 inhabitants in 2002	0.72	2.76	Wide gap, India lags
Compounded Annual Growth Rate (CAGR)* in main telephone lines over 1997-2002	16.4	24.3	Wide gap, India lags
IT per capita in 1999	15.4	37.9	Wide gap, India lags
Cellular subscribers as % of total telephone subscribers in 2002 — may be taken as an index to migration to wireless age like 4G.	23.4%	49.1%	Wide gap, India lags

Notes: India is found to be lagging behind china in almost all areas of it

Regional imbalances exist even within the developing zones.

* As per ITU, CAGR is calculated by the formula:

$[\{(V_p/V_0)^{(1/n)}\}-1] \times 100$; where V_p and V_o are respectively the present value and the beginning value, and n is the number of periods.

Leaving aside all reports and speculations, it is a hard fact that India lags behind China not only in the present context but also in the future wireless/mobile 4G ages.

1.5 DD WITHIN A COUNTRY

The picture of the DD at the global level, at the regional/zonal level has been examined. Within a country, the digital divide is a challenging social issue. The issue is not limited to the developing or the developed group. It is a global phenomenon. Therefore, we propose to analyze the figures of one country in this context. Hong Kong has been chosen for the purpose. In Table (1.6), a comparison of the positions of PCs in homes by household income, the use of PCs by educational attainment and the use of PCs by different age group and sex group is made. As per Thematic Household Survey[6] the Table shows that: (a) the percentage of PCs in homes increases with household income, (b) the use of PCs increases with educational level, (c) the use of PCs decreases with higher age group, and (d) the male users of PC are more

Table 1.6: Digital Divide in Hong Kong

Monthly household income in Hong Kong $	Rate (as a percentage of all households in the respective monthly household income group)	Age group	Rate of computer use by male	Rate of computer use by female
<10,000	15.3%	10-14	73%	72.8%
10,000 – 19,999	45.9%	15-24	76.1%	78.9%
20,000-29,999	62.8%	25-34	63.6%	65.0 %
30,000-39,999	70.7%	35-44	48.6%	44.5%
40,000-49,999	74.2%	45-54	25.2%	20.2%
>= 50,000	82.8%	55-64	9.1%	6.6%
		>= 65	1%	0.6%
Educational Attainment	Rate			
Secondary	52.3%			
Tertiary	89.5%			

Note: A survey under www.why-not.com/company/stats.htm, reports in 2004 that the world over gender statistics of Internet usages is as follows: Male = 61.5% and Female = 38.5%

than female user, with the exception that in the younger group the females either overtake or remain at par with males (of course, this is the global trend for younger generation).

Besides the parameters used above in studying the digital divide within a country (with Hong Kong as example), in all countries the digital divide exists in the urban-rural divide axis. The Table (1.7) illustrates a picture of several countries to this context[7]. The wide disparity between the urban and the rural docs never guarantee the social responsibility and achievement of any technology. The urban-rural divide on economic line is the rich-poor division. The technology must be so applied, so nurtured and so adopted so as to reduce the gap rather than increasing it.

Table 1.7: Telephone lines per 100 inhabitants in 1995 in few countries[8]

	Rural	Urban	Rural as percentage of Urban
Russia	8	20	40.00%
Moldova	6	23	25.00%
Georgia	3	18	16.66%
Ukraine	7	21	33.33%
Slovakia	11	28	39.30%
Albania	2	3	66.66%

1.6 DD IN LANGUAGE ZONE

The people speaking in their own language irrespective of the countries they belong to can share and exchange information for achieving benefits expected to get in the age of Internet, often known as global networked age. So a classification of the people on line in Internet access by language zone may be relevant. Table (1.8) gives a picture as per study[9]. It gives a picture of digital divide in the language zone, clearly giving an edge to English language.

1.7 LOOKING DIFFERENTLY

The sad disparities in different forms between the "haves" and the "have nots" in the current digital age have been clearly demonstrated in the above sections. The several reports and studies, on the other hand, established the very positive and active role of the IT in economic growth and development.

Table 1.8 (a): DD in language zone

Language	Internet access in million	% of world online population
English	287.5	35.8%
Total non-English	516.7	64.2%
Total European non-English	276	37.9%
Total Asian languages	240.6	33.0%
Total Scandinavian languages (Danish, Norwegian, Swedish, Iceland etc.)	14.6	2.0%
Russian	18.5	2.5%

Table 1.8 (b): Figures of 2002 as per www.cybertelecom.org

World Zone	Language	% Internet users by language	% Web content by language
	English	36% (44% as www. why-not.com)	69%
European other than English	Spanish	7%	2%
	German	7%	6%
	French	5%	3%
	Italian	4%	1%
Asian	Chinese	11%	4%
	Japanese	10%	6%
	Korean	5%	1%
Other		16%	9%

After several studies and researches, the dimensions of the transformations due to the information and the communication technologies have become clearer and widely understood. In broad terms, information and communication technologies advance and enhance all the aspects of economic, cultural, social and education life. The economic, social and education gap between poor and rich, rural and urban and man and woman is believed and understood to be narrowed down with infrastructure developments and accessibility of the informatics and the telematics. The UNESCO's Mac Bridge Commission[10] stated: "There can be no genuine, effective independence without the communication resources needed to safeguard it." Maitland Commission reported: "No development provision of any country should be regarded as balanced, properly integrated or effective without a full and appropriate role of telecommunication." GNP per person in US$ in 1994 was 24,290; 8,814 and 300 respectively in Japan, Taiwan and India, while the Internet users in thousand were respectively 3,500; 480 and 60 for these countries. The TV sets, the PCs and the CATV subscribers per 100 people were respectively 64.1, 12 and 8.3; 5.5, 0.1 and 1.1; and 31.5, 8.1 and 14.1 for these countries. These are enough indicators on international front about the positive role of information and communication technologies in the process of the developments. The same sort of picture has been noticed in India. The relative index of development and the teledensity in terms of % deviation from all India figures were –1% and –15%; –57% and –78%; +269% and +692%; +14% and +58% and –3% and –36% respectively for the states of Andhra Pradesh, Bihar (including Jharkhand), Delhi, Gujarat and West Bengal. The correlation between the development and the teledensity is well established in the noted figures. The deviation from the common trend is noticed only in case of Himachal Pradesh, which has allied figures of –25% and +53%. Except for a very few stray cases like that of the Himachal Pradesh, the appeal of the information and communication technologies in enhancing and improving developments is widely accepted. For substantially establishing the rosy picture of IT, the example of "grameen phone" of Bangladesh has brought immense economic benefits to rural inhabitants and the example of NDDB(National Dairy Development Board of India) initiatives to avoid the cheaters/ middlemen in milk business so that villagers can get the right price of their produce may be noted. It will be pertaining to mention here the world agencies reports[11,12] that the better communication enhances social and economic growth; the telecommunication provides benefit to cost ratio in the ranges from 5:1 to 100:1.

However, the rosy picture of IT for developments is clearly tilted towards the developed economies, as did the technologies of immediate past industrial age. The developing countries are to borrow and import IT technologies causing flow of resources and money from the Third World into the developed world. To this problem, there has been added one more, surely new in nature, in the IT age. Before and in 70s, raw materials were used to export from the developing/Third World to the developed world, and the value added or finished products were used to import into the Third World from the developed world. But with new technologies in hand, the developed countries are increasing the substitution of raw materials. The atomic/ nuclear power generation has to a great extent diminished the importance and the economics of OPEC countries. Whereas in the IT age, as the bits can be transported in thousands and thousands within a second in networks, there is no reason to import raw material in developed countries. This is becoming the rule of IT business. As such the World business has been gradually becoming more and more unidirectional in favor of the developed nations.

Added to the injury of the Third World is the present dictated globalization that has a single dimension of business. The current model of globalization is not either whole or full or total. Federio Mayor of UNESCO[13] told: "Globalization must never remain confined to only the networks, telecommunication, computers, the media world or markets. It will have to be based on the consolidation of a public democratic space worldwide. It is only on this condition that we will succeed in rendering globalization humane, making it a project with truly universal promise and giving it a meaning." Tagore's philosophy of: "One village and one country – that is world" in spirit of true globalization will be realized when any people in the world will answer in a common voice to a question "where do you live", that "I live in world." Till this is reached, three-fourths of world population that live in the developing countries will have to go with one-eighth of world's output and the developed countries will continue to enjoy and comfort with the rest of the nations. Mute question, then, remains: How do the developing countries cope with such huge disparity, imbalance and wide gap? The question is a million dollar question in view of the fact that the technology is changing in leaps and bound.

"Change" is the only thing that remains constant in the universe, whereas "creation, mastery and utilization of modern science and technology are basically what distinguish the South from the North[14]." Besides, the political nature of technology works heavily for its social entrepreneurship. Therefore, the developing countries must not just ignore or cannot afford to ignore any new technology, particularly IT in current perspective, but have to adopt it for judicious and intelligent applications rather than "hope of rising" based unplanned uses, which Dr. Colombo[15] put in as: "The ability of developing countries to derive all the benefits of the new technologies faces one stumbling block right from the start. Although rapidly and seemingly effortlessly permeating the economic and production systems of the world, these technologies are not available 'off the peg'. They have to be absorbed, metabolized, mastered and controlled. Their applications call for a pre-existing capability to insert new ideas, new practices, and new elements into a flexible system. This does not simply exist in the vast majority of the developing countries." The cost of a computer in Bangladesh is fifty times that of the average monthly income of a Bangladeshi, whereas USA it is in that of the average weekly income of an American. In such a sad scenario the developing countries have to design flexible systems for IT access and application for developments, for which the governments have to take initiatives and to this there appears no alternative.

The fact is that IT adds to economic developments and benefits, but the IT in an appropriate shape has not reached the rural and right people at the right application form resulting the DD to grow in volume and dimension. *Recognizing change as the essence of existence does not mean that we have to accept all changes. Being the master of change, we will know 'where to exploit change' and 'where the opportunities.'*

Several proposals in this context are suggested for possible consideration by policy makers of the developing countries in general and India in particular. This is based on the fact that whatever gap and whatever challenge, to be met are revolves around three factors: (i) economic and social gap, (ii) education gap, and (iii) status gap between agriculture and industry.

1.8 COMMUNITY INFORMATICS

There is a fundamental difference between invention and innovation. Innovation is the art of practical application of invention for development and productivity. The developing countries need to apply innovation for IT application, the beginning of which may be the development of community information center in the rural areas. The rural development shall be one of the most important applications to derive benefits of IT. The community information will have to be used for providing the IT access training, education for rural mass to benefit them as consumers, producers and citizen and particularly for farmers in context of market information (the agriculture producers must have the direct knowledge to get actual price of the produces), weather information and crop information (fertilizer, livestock, local production, etc.). The developing countries are agriculture and labour intensive, and that is how IT application needs innovations like community informatics. An environment needs to be created where IT must go to the rural masses en block by the government initiative rather than rural people coming to IT. This may be achieved by engaging educated unemployed youths for imparting mobile IT training in rural India. The areas not covered by electricity must not be left out but the technique of solar powered computer system may be employed. The community informatics may be directed to: (i) marketing benefits, (ii) increasing productivity of home made technologies/ appropriate technologies, (iii) mass education and training, and (iv) small business initiatives. The deprived group, the disadvantaged communities, and the rural masses must be given state sponsored opportunities to use IT for their economic and developmental benefits, before using computers to replace type-writers in offices.

1.9 INDUSTRIAL BARGA IN LINE WITH AGRICULTURAL BARGA

The existing economic and social gap between rich and poor is primarily due to two avalanche affects:

(a) In agriculture sector, negative avalanche is "produce and perish" and

(b) In business sector, positive avalanche is "produce and flourish".

One of the possible solutions may be to bring a balance between the prices of agriculture produce and that of business produce by strict control by governments. Mac Bridge Commission reported that the farmer and the agriculture producers must have the direct market knowledge to get actual price of the produces. This is believed to be possible only with IT.

1.9.1 Further Analysis on Industrial Barga

In history of social studies one important component of research deals with the findings of reasons and causes of growing gap between the rich and the poor and for that purpose to suggest measures and steps to reduce the gap. But the fact remains that the gap has not been reduced even after thousands of such studies and the implementation of their recommendations including of some noble laureates.

A few research findings report

1. If the present growth trends in world population, industrialization, pollution, food production, and resource depletion continue unchanged, the limits to growth on this planet will be reached sometime within the next 100 years. The most probable result will be a sudden and uncontrollable decline in both population and industrial capacity.
2. It is possible to alter these growth trends and to establish a condition of ecological and economic stability that is sustainable far into the future. The state of global equilibrium could be designed so that the basic material needs of each person on earth are satisfied and each person has an equal opportunity to realize his or her individual human potential.
3. If the people of the world decide to strive for this second outcome rather than the first, the sooner they begin working to attain it, the greater will be their chances of success.

To us those conclusions spelled do not put doom but challenge—how to bring about a society that is materially sufficient, socially equitable, and ecologically sustainable, and one that is more satisfying in human terms than the growth-obsessed society of today.

Whatever gap and whatever challenge is to be met revolves around three factors : (i) economic and social gap, (ii) education gap, and (iii) status gap between agriculture and industry.

Case of industries

The state of West Bengal in India has achieved a considerable amount of rural economic growth in the last two decades. The average income of the rural people has increased and the social security of rural people has been established on the solid footings. The disparity in income among the rural people has decreased considerably. An all-round development of rural people and society has been noticed. However, this development is due to land reforms and "barga" system sincerely implemented by the Left-front Government of West Bengal in their 25 years of rule.

By the process of land reforms and barga system, the agricultural workers or farmers are given confidence that they will never be thrown out of work and land they cultivate. This confidence has led to generate among farmers the more sense of belonging and sincerity in their work. This has reduced the victimization and the injustice meted out to them in terms of payment or no advance payment by the landlords—which in other ways has caused the agricultural productivity to increase and loss of agricultural working days to decrease as well as the agricultural disputes between labour and owner to lessen. The barga solution is our own and is not something copied from the developed nations.

The economic and productivity failures in all sectors namely agricultural, industrial and banking are mainly due to disputes between labours and owners. Thus, if such disputes in agriculture sectors are overcome by the barga system, it is logically extensible for other sectors like industrial and banking too. In this paper we propose an "industrial barga" system for Indian industries. We have achieved something unique by our own system of bargas in agriculture sector. Similarly, the industrial barga not prevailing elsewhere does not mean it is inappropriate in India. In Indian environment where economic disparity is huge and where labour is cheap and for which victimization of labour is easy, the industrial barga will be the right solution.

The proposed industrial barga aims to provide share of production and profit of industries with labour, management and owner as in agricultural barga. There may be several means of implementation. The industrial barga will not be easy to implement. We will illustrate a scheme of implementation with an example. In the technical contributions of man, machine, money and materials are measured in terms of money with salary, cost, etc. as equivalents. For example, say a company owned by Mr. Alice employs employees for a factory. Mr. Alice has established the factory at a total cost of Rs. 4 crore on land, buildings, equipments, etc. and the factory has the record of running cost as shown in Table (1.9). Thus over a year total spending equals to Rs. 459 lac and say the profit is Rs. 50 lacs. Hence this profit has to be shared as shown in the last column of Table (1.9) in the process of implementing industrial barga.

With IT age, the difference gap is easily to meet with. In the paper we have suggested two techniques to remove gaps of agriculture and industry sectors.

Table 1.9: Recod of Runnig Cost

	Position/Items	Money Equivalency in Rs.	Share to be given
A.	Initial non-recurring	4 crore (400 lac)	43.5729847 lac
B.	Salary (Recurring Annual Cost)/ Raw Materials		
(a)	Mr. Alice	18 lacs	1.9607843 lac
(b)	CEO	6 lacs	0.653594766 lac
(c)	Manager	4 lacs	0.435729844 lac
(d)	Deputy/Asst. Manager	3 lac (1.5 lac.each)	0.098039215 lac
(e)	Supervisors	3 lac (1 lac each)	0.098039215 lac
(f)	Office staff	1.2 lac (40,000 each)	0.130718954 lac
(g)	Labours	0.8 lac (20,000 each)	0.087145969 lac
(h)	Raw Material Required	20 lac	2.178649237 lac

The proposed industrial barga aims to provide share of production and profit of industries with labor, management and owner as in agricultural barga. There may be several means of implementation. The industrial barga will not be easy to implement. A scheme of implementation illustrated in this regard may be used.

1.10 RESHAPING EDUCATION/I-C-I: OUR SOLUTION IN OUR WAYS

"Without improved human capital, countries will inevitably fall behind and experience intellectual and economic marginalization and isolation. In the developed world education is a major political priority."—UNESCO. Education at all levels is imperative for all-round development of any nation and it has become more and more important in the present age of competitive globalised economy guided by emerging technologies[16-19]. Education being the basic and main backbone of a nation, undoubtedly is a component of social infrastructure that the government must liberally invest in, besides controlling and monitoring as well as raising the quality of education. The improved human resource generation has been tested over history and proved beyond doubt, as the sound strategy for competitive advantage, yet the poor and developing nations under compulsion and resource crunch fail to fully implement the strategy. The developing countries in general face acute problem of funding the high cost of higher education. It has several dimensions:

- Due to high cost of higher education, although high cost involved in higher education is a debatable issue on several aspects, the developing countries fail to increase the number of higher educational institutes causing percentage of availability of higher education per people decreasing.
- The stated decrease in percentage as above is compounded multifold due to high increase in enrolment ratio with growing population. The enrolment in tertiary education in India in 1970, 1985 and 1995 was respectively 4.9%, 6.0% and

6.5%. India ranked 141 out of 173 countries in the overall education index in the year 2000. India ranks below even most developing countries in terms of enrolment per 100,000 inhabitants.

- The imposition of globalized economy has several restrictions on investment on higher education forcing the developing and poor countries to further fall behind in higher education scenario. At the same time, given the current scenario, no government is able to pull out of globalization.
- It is an irony that the developing countries in order to compete with the developed nations, blindly try to copy or follow the higher education system/structure of the developed nations. The natural consequences happen in the form of wide mismatch between the requirement, supply and demand, one component of which is seen in the brain drain or reluctant brain drain. This causes the return on investment to decrease that acts heavily behind the investment by government.
- It is most unfortunate that the pattern of investment in the higher educational institutes/universities lack merits causing many great universities/institutes not getting grants as appropriate or productive based, whereas other low productive based universities/institutes getting higher share of budget. This causes the negative avalanche in the productive growth of the higher education.
- Due to GATT adoption that is next natural step of globalization, the private initiatives in higher education have been noticed at the developing countries. But several studies have clearly demonstrated the huge imbalance in the process that may be counter-productive.

Our prolonged exercise in copying/adopting the developed countries, in cheap labour and in the generation of third largest technical manpower has proved wrong. They have neither brought any meaningful results nor any relief in any form. It is undoubtedly true that our achievements in academic and basic scientific research are internationally recognized yet we need to import telecommunication switches, PCs, and air crafts. We are called software giant, yet till date no system software like DOS, WINDOWS, and Unix could we originate. This clearly speaks for the wide gap between academic and industry that is clearly absent in the developed countries. **Our failure to lead "Invention to Innovation" is the root cause** for the continuous lag. This is not identified today, but long back. Even Kothari Commission argued for the Institute-Industry interaction, but till date no concrete and meaningful interaction has been achieved.

Now-a-days the industries are opening universities. We need to explore the possibilities of universities opening industries. The two-way bridges are more flexible and surely competitive, rather than one-way bridge. Therefore, a new solution in our form for a solid collaboration is the need of the hour. In this context, the concept of "ICI" (Institute-cum-Industry) with FARE and SARE[20-23] is a powerful solution.

The implementation of ICI must be based on several strategies: (a) It should aim Future Objectives and Keys (FOAK) both for academic programs and industrial production, because we badly need a quantum jump to come ahead in the race in coming days, (b) No failure must be discouraged, as failures add experience to the venture, (c) Short-term Return on Investment (ROI) must be forgotten forever, wait for 6 to 10 years, (d) The research centers must be taken as profit rather than cost centres, (e) Perceptions should not overrule reality, and (f) Doers and not makers must be rewarded.

1.11 CONCLUSION

There is an urgent need to realize DIGITAL DIVIDEND (DIVIDE + END) in order to utilize the opportunities and scope that the emerging technology has to offer. The DIVIDEND is to raise the voices of the poor, the deprived, the oppressed and the disadvantaged society and then only the technology will justify its due role on social dimension. For this act, the policy-makers have to stop techniques of copying ideas of the developed countries, that has been time tested by now as an exercise of complete futility. Individual country must have to address their own problems in their socio-economic fabric before applying technology. For a country like India, the suggestions of state sponsored community informatics for rural masses, the introduction of industrial barga for rural labours, and the ICI type education system appear vision based solutions, although the suggestion may generate public debate and constructive criticism. The work gives a message to the Third World/developing countries. The message is portrayed below:

Want to be a Leader in Knowledge Age?

Yes → 1, 2, 3 below

No → Go to Hell

1. GO for Community Informatics in a massive way
2. GO for Industrial Barga
3. GO for ICI, and FARE and SARE and integrated courses

To become a world player, a nation needs to attain three critical masses in the areas of information uses and consumption (CMIUC), economic and financial confidence (CMEFC) and higher and highly skilled technical manpower(CMHST) which are believed to be achieved respectively by massive community informatics projects **coupled with e-learning application in massive way,** industrial barga and modified education system of higher technical education (ICI). A fair estimate of the figures of critical masses would be: (a) 50% of whole national population for CMIUC out of which 80% and 50% may be over urban and rural population respectively (in India 20% population lives in urban areas and 80% of this will constitute about 16% over national population. Similarly, 80% Indian population is rural and its 50% will mean about 40%. Thus 16% + 40%, together may lead to about 50% desired critical mass), (b) 80% of industrial labours for CMEFC in compliance with the claimed 80% achievement in agricultural barga in West Bengal, and (c) 10% of national population in CMHST without any separate distribution over urban and rural population as because the inherent ability and geniusness to become skilled technical manpower do not depend on geographical area, caste and creed. A nation needs to achieve the critical masses in shortest possible time for competitive advantages in the open and liberalized world. The shortest possible time should be at most a five-year period.

Before the final end of this section, I would like to note a few questions for the future research as shown in the Table (1.10).

Table 1.10: Unanswered questions

Agricultural Barga is an excellent achievement	But is Barga for agriculture or agriculture for Barga?	Why is there no Industrial Barga?
Technical Education in LPG in India	Private investment in education or privatized education?	
Networks in improving education	Replacement or supplement?	I have a suggestion as told in the section 4.4 on e-learning

Notes

1. Steven M. Cherry, "A World Divided by a Common Internet", *IEEE Spectrum*, Feb. 2004, pp. 50-51.
2. http://www.internetworldstats.com.
3. World Development Indicators Database, World Bank, April 2004.
4. World Telecommunication Indicators, ITU, December 2003.
5. World Development Indicators, 2003.
6. Hong Kong Computer Society Paper on Digital Divide in Hong Kong.
7. *Mac Bridge Commission Report* of World Bank.
8. *World Telecommunication Development Report*, ITU, 1998.
9. http://global-reach.biz/globstats.
10. *Mac Bridge Commission Report* of World Bank.
11. *Ibid.*
12. *Maitland Commission Report*, ITU, Geneva, 1984.
13. Tibor Braun, Wolfgang Glanzel and Andras Schubert, "A Global Snapshot of Scientific Trends", *UNESCO Courier*, May, 1999, pp. 28-29.
14. Dr. Colombo, "The Technological Revolution and the Future of the Third World", *IEEE Technology & Society Magazine*, Spring, 1991, pp. 25-32.

15. *Ibid.*
16. Gerardo R. Ungson and John D. Trudel, "The Emerging Knowledge-Based Economy", *IEEE Spectrum,* May, 1999, pp. 60-65.
17. Constantine N. Anagnostopolous and Lauren A. Williams, *Few Gold Stars for Pre-college Education,* April, 1998, pp. 18-26.
18. C.T. Bhunia, "Person Power Development—Why and How", *CSI Communication*, 1996, pp. 7-11.
19. C.T. Bhunia et al., "Technical Education and Training for the Information Age, *J. Productivity*, Vol. 39, No. 4, 1999, pp. 579-587.
20. C.T. Bhunia, "Institute Cum Industry—A New Model for Technical Education", *University News*, August 29, 1994, pp. 11-14.
21. C.T. Bhunia et al., "Model Structure of ICI of Electronics and Computer Engineering", Proc ISTE National Seminar, Feb. 14-15, 1995, pp. 1-11.
22. C.T. Bhunia, "Higher Education—Restructuring", *J University News,* Jan. 2000, pp. 1-4.
23. C.T. Bhunia, "Overcoming High Costs of Higher Education", *J University News,* June 2003, pp. 6-12.

References

C.T. Bhunia, "Knowledge Management: Why & How", *JIETE*, Vol. 21, No. 1, Jan-Feb. 2004, pp. 25-37.

C.T. Bhunia, IT: An Enginee Proc. 19th National Seminar of IE (I), 2004, Patna, pp. 61-70.

Goldman Website, "dreaming with BRIC: the path to 2050."

The Would-be Strategy for the Developing/Poor Nations to Take Part in the Globalization Process

2

2.1 STUDIES FROM OPTIMISTIC VIEWS OF GLOBALIZATION OR INFORMATION AGE

On the eve of 21st century, the world is witnessing the emergence of the knowledge revolution. This is the true impact of third wave, the computer. Last half of the last century was shaped by a single most technology known as Information Technology. Information Technology is the fruit of the marriage of the computer and the communication. This marriage heralded the end of the industrial age dominated by machines and engines, automobiles and textile mills; and builds the foundation of the information age or the knowledge society. The new knowledge age is distinctly separate from the machine age in several aspects:

- **Shift from science-aspect to human-aspect production/ From machine to knowledgeable man:** The industrial age was limited to science-based means of production[1]. Machines were assumed as the main source of production using energy and raw materials. The information age accepts the social and the human aspect of production. Human ingenuity, "know-how" and "state of the art" are assumed as the main sources of productive capability in knowledge age. Owen's virtual machines with knowledge are the most resourceful sources in the new economic based society of present days.
- **Shift from money, material, man to knowledge:** On the emergence of the new economy order of the present days, Peter Drucker[2] argued that "knowledge

is not just another resource that adds to the traditional [factors of] labour, land and capital – it is the only meaningful resource today." Today, knowledge is key. Knowledge is power. Knowledge is saleable. He also said, "The proper or improper use of different factors of production depends upon the wishes of human resources. Hence, besides other resources, human resources need more development". Bhaskar Dutta[3] observed that "soon knowledge rather than capital and machinery will be the key input", in developments.

- **Shift to a new source of wealth:** A report[4] says, "Information Technology has (also) produced a new source of wealth that is not material; it is information – knowledge applied to work to create value."
- **Shift from local to global:** Communication and flood of real time data transfer, world over, have transformed the international economy in several aspects. Unlike industrial age, location of raw materials is unimportant today. It is said[5] if we can transfer bits of information, there is no need of shipment of raw materials. Global connectivity pursues global scope of activities, production and business ensuring production and business from anywhere to anywhere at anytime.
- **Shift from quantity to quality:** Quality and Innovation are key factors of productivity in present age. "Innovate and Flourish" is the main mantra. This is because[6] "when we apply knowledge to ongoing tasks, we increase productivity. When we apply it to new tasks, we create innovation. The pursuit of wealth is now largely the pursuit of information and its application to the means of production."
- **Shift to presence of everywhere:** Unlike industrial age, the machines of information age namely, computer and communication are used everywhere—in factories,

in schools, in colleges, in offices, in homes, in societies, in shops, etc. The application is wide and vast.

These changes were classified into 17 groups by Yoneji Masuda[7]. The changes he described are as follows:

A. Technological Change:

1. **Change in core or prime technology and their basic functions:** The prime technology of industrial age was the steam engine, and "its major function was substitute for and amplify the physical labour of man". The main technology of the knowledge society in the computer and its fundamental function is "to substitute for and amplify the mental labour man".
2. **Change in productive power:** The industrial age brought the revolution in "material productive power (increase in per capita production)". The mass production of goods and their rapid transportation and services were the motive of the age. The information age is to expand information productive power (increase in optimal action/selection capabilities), and make possible "the mass production of cognitive, systematized information, technology and knowledge.

B. Socio-economic Structure:

3. **Change in modern factory**: In industrial age, the modern factory or production center was made of heavy machines and equipments. In the information age, the computers, the networks' connectivity and data banks shall form the production and distribution center for information goods.
4. **Change in market:** In the industrial age, market expanded due to the discovery of new continents and the acquisition of colonies. The main factor in the expansion of market was the increase in consumption power. In the information age, "the knowledge – frontier" will become the potential market.
5. **Change in leading industries:** In the information age, the intellectual industries, the knowledge industries

and the information industries shall replace the machinery and the chemical industries, which were the leading industries of industrial age.

6. **Change in economic structure:** The economic structure of the industrial age was characterized by: (i) a sales-oriented commodity economy, (ii) specialization of production utilizing divisions of labour, (iii) complete division of production and consumption between enterprise and household. The economic structure of the information age shall be characterized by: (i) information utility, (ii) self-production of information, and (iii) synergetic economy (joint production and shared utilization). There shall be a shift from exchange economy to synergetic economy.
7. **Change in socio-economic principle:** The industrial age in characterized by the universal law of price, which establishes the equilibrium of supply and demand. It maintains the economic order. The information age shall be characterized by the law of goals (principle of synergetic feed forward is supposed to maintain the order of the society.)
8. **Change in socio-economic subject:** There are as of social activity in industrial age the private enterprises, public enterprises and government enterprises. In the information age, a new social group like voluntary communities (local and informal communities) shall arise.
9. **Change in socio-economic system:** The socio-economic system of the industrial age was a system of private ownership of capital, free competition and profit maximization. In the information age, "the socio-economic system will be a voluntary civil society characterized by the superiority of its infrastructure, as a type of both public capital and knowledge-oriented human capital, and by a fundamental framework that embodies the principle of synergy and social benefit".

10. **Change in form of society:** Industrialized society was a society of centralized power and control and hierarchical classes. Information society shall be functional society and autonomous society.
11. **Change in national goal:** The national goal of information age shall be GNS (Gross National Satisfaction) unlike GNW (Gross National Welfare) of industrialized age. Realization of time values is another goal of information age.
12. **Change in form of Government:** The industrialized age was characterized by parliamentary system and majority rule. The information age shall be characterized by participatory democracy. Citizen's participation and opinions shall be characterized by participatory democracy. Citizen's participation and opinions shall be major in running the government.
13. **Change in social force:** In industrial age, the labour unions were the major force for social changes. In the information age, citizen movements will be the force behind social changes.
14. **Change in social problems**: In industrial age there were three main groups of social problems: "recession-induced unemployment, wars resulting from international conflicts, and the dictatorship of fascism." In the information age, the social problems shall be "shocks caused by the inability of the people to respond smoothly to rapid societal information, acts of individual and group terrorists" such as "invasions of individual privacy and the crisis of a controlled society."
15. **Change in most advanced stage:** "The most advanced stage of industrial society is a high mass consumption stage, centering on durable goods, as evidenced by motorization (the diffusion of the automobile). The most advanced stage of the information society will be the high mass knowledge creation society in which computerization will make it possible for each person to create knowledge and to go on to self fulfilment."

C. Values, Ethick and Spirits:

16. **Change in values and ethics standards:** The industrial age was characterized by material values (satisfaction of physiological and physical needs) and fundamental human rights and humanity. The information age shall be characterized by time value (satisfaction of achieved goals), self-discipline and social contribution.
17. **Change in spirit:** The spirit of the industrial age was human liberation "which ethically means respect for fundamental rights and a spirit of brotherly love to rectify inequalities." The spirit of information society shall be globalism and universalism, a symbiosis of man and nature.

As per Rada[8] main areas of impact of IT are as below:

A. Effect in production:

1. Substitution of mechanical components, electro-mechanical components, electric and older electronics.
2. Upgradation of traditional products and controls.

   New products.

B. Effect in manufacturing process:

1. Use of CAD/CAM – increase in the flexibility, adaptability and economy of production.
2. CNC machines and Robots – incorporation of skills and function into equipments.

C. Effect in offices:

1. Automation of routine clerical work.
2. Increase in the efficiency and effectiveness of communications.

D. Effect in services:

1. Transportability of services – remote access to databases, banks etc. This also leads to new services.
2. Increase in self-service.

But on pessimistic side, Rada, urged "the industrial utilization of IT leads to an erosion of developing countries' comparative advantages and international competitiveness, especially in traditional industries." The reasons as per Rada are:

(i) Decrease in the relative importance of labour-intensive manufacturing and cost of labour.
(ii) Changes in product Cycles.
(iii) Quality consideration.

Table 2.1: Manufacturing Cost Per Device (US$)

Process	Hong Kong	US
Manual	0.0248	0.0753
Semi-automatic	0.0183	0.0293
Automatic	0.0163	0.0178

Source : *Global Electronics Information Newsletter*, No. 25, October 1982.

Table 2.2: Computerization of the Postal Check System in Algeria, 1974-77

	Manual 1974	Computerized 1977
No. of operations	24,360,000	33,620,000
Volume (millions DA)	109.5	210.8
No. of accounts	452,000	709,000
Waiting time at centers before processing of document	15 days	2 days
Payment at cash desk	3-6 hours	2 min
Saturation ratio	95%	50%
Employment	856	680

Source: Secretariat d'Etat au Plan, Commissariat National a l' Informatique, "L'Informatique en Algerie", Algiers, 1978.

Table 2.3: Worldwide Telecommunications Equipment Market* (US $1000)

	1980	%	1985	%	1990	%
Developed countries	36	90	53.5	89	75.4	86
Developing countries	4	10	6.7	11	12.1	14
Total	40	100	60.2	100	87.5	100

Note:*Includes telephone, telegraph, telex, data communications, satellite communications, mobile radio and radio telephone, radio paging, and cable TV.

Source : Arthur D. Little Inc.

Table 2.4: Transmission and Satellite Markets (US$ million)

Continent	Telegraph, Telex & Satellite			
	Data transmission		Communications	
	1980	1990	1980	1990
Africa	48.4	97.3	3.0	10.5
Latin America	106.5	189.0	14.3	34.9
North America	2481.4	6000.0	122.8	463.7
Europe	733.9	1984.1	59.0	189.2

Source : Arthur D. Little Inc.

The benefits of IT are immense. The benefits relate to economical benefits and societal benefits:

1. The computer-assisted production has a higher rate of productivity.
2. The cost of the computer-assisted production is less.
3. The production becomes independent of location of raw materials.
4. IT has reduced "NO TIME" problem. Efficient use of time is possible with application of IT in hand; "swift movement of capital and slow movement of people" have added flexibility, efficiency and effectiveness in business towards globalization process. Richard S. Sloma in his book, *No Nonsense Management* observed, "Your true adversary is time." The impact of IT application on time or mobility of managers can be defined by an equation: Volume of information available on managers' desk × Volume of mobility of managers = Constant.

   The stated equation means, more is the information available on the desk less is the required mobility of management. IT provides competitive advantages in business and economy. Today, not only better, but also faster has become another parameter of success. In a real sense, the advantage is titled towards those who are using IT in their work, activities and business.
5. IT offers improved HRD. As per *Bhagvad Gita*, HRD as a system is made of two sub systems: (i) Karmyog

where Sadhana proceeds along the path of action, and (ii) Sankhayog where it follows along the path of knowledge. Vivekananda's "karma is dharma" is Karmayog that comes out of the knowledge, which, "is the perfection already in man." Sankhyya comes of the information available to a human.

One total human is a sum total of the physical self, the emotional self and the intellectual self. IT has a direct impact in enhancing the intellectual self of a human being. HRD concerns with training, education and development. Training provides sharpening of capabilities and skill required to perform the present job. Education refers to acquisition of knowledge for further job, and it is a means of change. Development refers to improvement of an individual to earn the capabilities, experiences and leadership to cope up with changes and the new directions of the organization. IT has introduced teleteaching, telescopic courses and audio-video cassettes to deal with training and education at home or at office, at individual effort and at organizational level. This has made HRD process more cost-effective, time controlled, conformable and easier.

"Survival of the fittest" – is the slogan of the present age of global competition and liberalized open economy. Four mantras for being and keeping fittest are[9]:

- Improved Human Resources to lead,
- Global Information on Desk to guide
- Innovate to flourish, and
- Quality to nourish.

Assume a nation to be a car. To drive this car, first two mantras are respectively the driver and the fuel. Last two mantras are the directions and driving.

Schumpeter[10] made a fundamental distinction between invention and innovation. To his notion, invention is the discovery of new techniques and process and innovation is the practical application of invention for marketable production. Invention refers to Sankhyayog, whereas innovation refers to

Karmayog. Scientists and technologists do the invention and entrepreneurs do the innovation.

In reference to the need of the information age, UNESCO's MacBride commission stated: "There can be no genuine, effective independence without the communication resources needed to safeguard it."

2.1.1 What is the Economic Growth Theory of Age of IT?

Any economic growth theory is to identify the capital. Adam Smith told that the engine of economic growth is the accumulation of capital. In the age of Adam Smith the capital was money and the economic growth was accumulation of money and division of labour. In the industrial age, the capital was management, which is a set of man, money, machine and materials. In the information age, the capital is knowledge. The economic growth theory of the age of IT is the accumulation of knowledge rather than man, money, materials and machine.

The logical and obvious conclusion that can be made from the technology trend shown above is:

If the third world countries want to take part in globalization process, they have to go for knowledge and skill.

2.2 STUDIES ON FACTS AND FIGURES/FROM PESSIMISTIC VIEWS OF THE GLOBALIZATION OR INFORMATION AGE

(A) Entering into the world of liberation

— The case of Third World —

Tagore once told, "we have only one country in this universe, and that is world." Rabindranath Tagore's such a powerful philosophy may ultimately be realized if today's tenet of "one world one village is implemented in true sense in future. What has happened to the deployment of computer in government sectors in India today is anybody's guess. This is a lesson that the Third World always forgets. Consequently, the Third World continues to lag behind International trends, and loses money as there is hardly any planning for technological up gradation and applications. We can sight a figure to justify this point. Telecommunications lines of India are 66% digitized; whereas figures of Brazil and Hungary are respectively 35.7%

and 41%. But the faults figures are 218 faults per 100 lines in India and 2 faults per 100 lines in USA and Japan. Better is not the sole dimension of competitive advantages; faster is equally another important dimension. Thus it will be a sound strategy for the developing countries to take part in the globalization without any further loss of time, but with intelligent, selective, judicious and strategic applications of globalization process, uses of and innovation with few technologies. Analyzing the problems of Third World in depth Dr. Colombo observed, "The ability of developing countries to derive all the benefits of the new technologies faces one stumbling block right from the start. Although rapidly and seemingly effortlessly permeating the economic and production systems of the world, these technologies are not available "off the peg". They have to be absorbed, metabolized, mastered and controlled. Their application calls for a pre-existing capability to insert new ideas, new practices, and new elements into a flexible system. This does not simply exist in the vast majority of the developing countries. Furthermore, it is essential that as the new technologies are introduced into the socio-economic fabric of the Third World, they do not impair or destroy existing local cultures.... We must equally concern ourselves with safeguarding the richness of the world cultures, mankind's "cultural genoma." Despite these problems I strongly believe that the intelligent application of the new technologies in the developing countries can indeed speed up the process of economic growth." Let me allow to express my observation pertaining to what I mean by intelligent use of globalization process. In India, we need privatization and globalization in the sectors of telecommunication, power, railways and information technologies but certainly not in the sector of chicken curry. Welcoming globalization process in the telecommunication sectors but restricting the foreign participation to only 25% is a mere and laughed-at fallacy. On the other hand, by the name of globalization, allowing business in and with education and learning is wrong not only on social and ethical grounds but also on strategic and developmental reasons. For developing countries to go with liberalization we must distinct three things: Education (including higher education and research), Agriculture and Infrastructure (EAI); and separately justify how to go with them to implement a true and Third World's friendly liberalization, globalization and privatization process. Noted economist Professor Amartya Sen termed education and health as the social infrastructure, whereas transport, power and communication as physical infrastructures. Criticizing the present form of India's liberalization process he observed, "there are documents which emphasize only these physical infrastructures, and not the social infrastructures like education and health. And that's a mistake too." We can examine in the article how the Third World countries proceed with three things, EAI in the process of privatization and globalization.

Professor Amartya Sen[11] pointed out that there are two types of experiences of globalization process; Brazil's way, which has extremely unequal development, and South Korea's way where there has more widely spread development. Professor Sen cautioned India against going in Brazil's way. For the success of liberalization, he advised India to go in South Korea's way. No Third World country can ignore this strategic advice of Professor Sen. For equal growth developing countries must look into social sectors, which include agriculture, education and health. Professor Sen warned that unequal growth leads to a situation "which is social counter-productive and economically counter-productive." Third World countries are rural based countries. Agriculture is the main and the only source of means for the vast rural masses of these countries. Rural masses of these countries constitute about 80% of the vast population. Food, health and basic education are the three minimum social needs for a human being to live with. In rural areas, children are forced to give up education due to poverty. On the other hand, health is a consequence of poverty. It is apparent that with elimination of rural poverty, health and education are likely to improve. Going for liberalization and for hi-fi technology without solving the basic problems of rural poverty, shall be a wrong decision and it will never bridge the gap between nation's "fear of falling" and "hope of rising." Third World countries must first try to improve the agriculture sector and that shall have to do with 100% governmental control and financial assistance. In India we have the experience of governmental controlled and aided first green revolution each after, if not less than but at least a 20 years gap to meet with the problem of poverty, and this may eventually emerge as a permanent solution. This will be the first and foremost priority of governments of Third World countries.

Education in general, and Science and Technological education (including research) in particular should be given a new look in Third World countries. Today knowledge is power. Knowledge is saleable. Knowledge is industry. KASO — Knowledge, Attitude, Skills and Others are the weapons of industrial prosperity and social enlistment. Human resource development has become the top priority to managers. We had already seen Dr. Colombo's call for developing a pre-existing capability for new technologies. Computer Society of India has already given a call for "Person Power" development for IT revolution in India. Prof. Salam[12] told that, "..... Creation, mastery and utilization of modern science and technology is basically what distinguished the South from the North........if there is one lesson to be drawn from the second gulf war between Iraq and the allies, it is this: no amount of borrowed technology can compete with genuine home grown high technology." Intellectual abilities of the Third World countries are vast. But as of now, either these abilities are not being used in their respective countries or being used by the developed countries for their development at a very low cost or being misused in their respective countries. We have to use and tap these resources in proper means and with proper training and education. Besides, our education systems and structures are all copied from the developed nations, and therefore, there is a wide mismatch between what we need and what we are doing in education sectors. This is why we often feel our higher education is costly and that is why we fail to meet with the financial requirement of higher education. Third World countries badly need to change education systems and structures with following things in mind:

- production of highly skill oriented technical engineers rather than academic engineers.
- introduction of self-revenue generation scheme in institutes and universities for investment in R&D.
- developing measures to attract bright students into faculty and to stop brain drain.
- integrated approach in education system.
- removing prejudice and preference in education management.
- proper use of products of higher education, in planning and execution — in this regard it shall be a very right proposition to refer Dr. S. Basu's observation made in his article[13] that even within "in project specific matters" in government, "authority rests with bureaucracy" causing thereby returns of higher education to become marginal. In this regard we can sight different recommendations of different high power committees: (i) Administrative Reforms Committee (ARC) of Morarji Desai and K. Hanumanthaya recommended that "all posts in a functional area whether in field or in headquarters or in the secretariat should be staffed by members of the corresponding functional services....", (ii) ARC of W.B. headed by Dr. Asoke Mitra, MP, recommended that "the technical head, whether already holding the position of ex-officio secretary, or otherwise, should be formally designated as the secretary to the department....." Of course, later we shall see this practice may be coupled with open administration structure in order to attain maximum benefits.
- providing recognition of industrial status to the institutes of higher learning and education.

Developing countries need to have highly trained and skill oriented and innovative people. Today's success theory is IT—

Innovation and Training. Porter's model of success is "innovate or perish." This is possible[14] "if our people power are superior in terms of knowledge, know-how (Note: need of training, skill, etc.) and innovative capacity (Note: need of research and development). We have already seen that arguments based on the availability of highly qualified but cheap labour are untenable." Keeping all these in mind, we could suggest that Third World countries may go for designing ICI (Institute-cum-Industry)[15-18] type educational establishment. ICI could be based on modular[19] pattern of education. Out of the two departments of ICI namely, institute department and industry department, the role of industry department shall be to implement commercially viable projects in which students shall work as main technical workers. We must expect a group of final year diploma students of electronics and communication engineering to assemble a colour TV set in a commercial way. We must ask a group of M.Tech. students of electrical engineering to fully design a 1 MW hydel power station as their project. In these projects faculty members and other engineers shall be supervisors and students may act as workers. By this students shall get an environment of "learn while doing" or "learn by doing", and this shall help them to be better professionals. It will be pertaining to note here the theory of effectiveness of mode of teaching or training that the effectiveness is 20% of what we see, the effectiveness is 30% of what we hear, the effectiveness is 50% of what we hear and see and the effectiveness is 80% of what we see, hear and do. A Chinese proverb tells, "Tell me and I shall forget, show me and I shall remember, involve me and I shall understand." ICI shall bring highest effective mode of teaching and training. Teachers shall do research in real and practical laboratories and in real and practical environment rather than so-called research laboratories which are often artificial and virtual in nature. All practical classes and research shall be carried on in the industrial laboratories of ICI. ICI can bid farewell permanently to humiliated pay scales offered to professors and to the cries such as "state financing not possible for higher education" and "scientific grants are not giving matching returns", etc.

Mr. Edouard Balladuar, former French Prime Minister in his one of the articles, "At the crossroads"[20] noted that "everyone should have access to a general education, which is often the best way to acquire that range of diverse skills which enables people to adapt to future changes over the course of their lives. But our system of education should give more importance to technical and vocational training, and to ties with business." ICI is in spirit with this observation except that "business" is replaced with "industry".

Last but not least, is infrastructure. Infrastructure includes communication, information networks, road, transport, railways, etc. Communication is even called as infrastructure of infrastructures. We know that infrastructures are capital-intensive sectors. Governmental control may not be justified and affordable to in these sectors. We shall analyze in this paper the problem of Third World in respect of information and communication infrastructure. We have logic behind that choice. As per UNO, a country's development is measured by three indexes: country's GNP which is a measure of the country's economy in general, country's HDI which is the measure of the country's human resource development and whether the country is "information rich" or "information poor" which may be indexed by the ICI – Information Consumption Index. UNO has a means of calculating these, and they regularly publish these data. We shall try here to study these for a few selected countries and compare them for deriving a way out for infrastructure development of Third World countries. We have selected eight countries including six from Asia, one each from Europe and America. In Table (2.5-2.9)[21,22,23], we have shown some figures of these countries, which shall be used to calculate the normalized indexes: GNP, HDI, ICI and population index (PI). Mode of calculation of normalized index is shown in the respective tables. In case of HDI, we have considered % GNP spent by the respective countries on health and education as the parameters of measurement. For calculating ICI we have used TV sets, PCs, phone lines, CATV subscribers per 10 people in the respective countries. In Table (2.10) we have compared these figures for these eight countries. The "*" marked countries in Table (2.10) are the countries which are having GNP, HDI and ICI below the average of these eight countries, and which are having PI above the indexes of these eight countries. Thus "*" marked countries could be termed as third grade countries. It is unfortunate to note that in these respects India and China becomes "third in third" countries. Piquant position of India in ICI profoundly suggests us to do something positive for infrastructure development of information sectors, basically communication sectors of India. While figures speak for this, quality goes a step ahead. Even you dial a correct number, sometimes you hear "Please check the number you have dialled. There is no route corresponding to the number dialled by you", from Indian telephone. If you redial a number after half an hour after first getting a busy tone, you will be a lucky man if you do not hear again, "This line is busy, please dial after sometime, thank you." What is then? There is nothing but 100% privatization of this sector the need of the hour. For overall comparison we can define a ratio of average development index $[=(y_1 + y_2 + y_3)/3]$ to PI. This ratio of a country shall be like the signal to noise ratio of a communication system. In Table (2.11), we have shown the ratio for the 8 countries. We can notice the sorry figures of India and China. The reasons behind our poor ratio are: low ICI and high PI. The present state of communication sector is not only hampering our all round development, but also worst affecting us to become worst environmental hazard country in the world. For telecommunication reforms five key principles[24] often referred to are: private investment, competition, a flexible regulatory framework, open access and universal service. Developing countries cannot think otherwise. In India a survey was made on ATM development in India[25], and the result shows that for such deployment the majority of the respondents has accepted private participation. In[26] analyzing reforms policy of telecommunication sectors of developing countries it was shown the "key reforms objectives include increasing efficiency and autonomy, investment, and responsiveness to customers" and it is widely believed that these can be achieved by private initiatives in communication. A study[27] was made for information sector and their implications for developing countries. It was shown that information provides competitive advantages in terms of three factors: space, time and scale, enumerating the advantages of use of informatics in the developmental process, a few steps were suggested for information sectors of developing countries. There was also a mention of liberalization in information sectors.

In communication sector, government's role shall be limited only to licensing and regulatory authority. Regulatory and licensing board must be one open system where highest executives starting from joint secretary to chairman level should be filled on contract basis by appointment from outside government. Mr. S. Medullar, member of the Fifth Pay Commission, shall in spirit with suggestion recently put this forward. We should note that in a developed Asia-Pacific country, telecommunication revolution occurred during the tenure of a vice-chancellor as chairman of the telecommunication board of that country. Power revolution in West Bengal was brought by Hon' Power Minister Prof. Sankar Sen, a former vice-chancellor of Jadavpur University. Once upon a time, when West Bengal was a leader in education in India, its education secretary was Prof. D.M. Sen. After D.M. Sen, there has been no change, no innovation in West Bengal's education system, the result of which is that West Bengal is now at tenth or below in national listing of education in 1980s.

A number of studies[28,29] have revealed that better communication enhances social and economic growth, telecommunication provides benefit to cost ratio in the range from 5:1 to 100:1. It is reported that, "There can be no genuine, effective independence without the communication resources needed to safeguard it." Maitland Commission report suggested that, "No development provision of any country should be regarded as balanced, properly integrated or... effective without a full and appropriate role for telecommunications." Professor Amartya Sen[30] observed that "the development of the transport sector, power sector, communication, are extremely important both from the point of economic expansion as well as from the point of view of social change." A study[31] reveals, "telecommunications investments yield exceptionally high returns to the economy as a whole. Ten recent telecommunications development programs partly financed by the World Bank in a number of countries, for example, are expected to yield on an average at least 18% economic rate of return, or 37% when conservative measures of consumer surplus are added. These figures are well in excess of the 10-14% marginal returns in the overall economics." In[32] it was shown how essential and effective is the communication in case of disasters. In[33] the chicken and egg relationship was referred to the equation between telecommunication investment and economic growth. It was shown that "the economic impact is comparatively greater in regions with low telephone density (i.e. rural and remote areas)." Thus benefits of communication shall not be prerogative of elite society. Even in case of multimedia communication Linda, Clinton White House Education Advisor[34] observed, "we must make sure that the Information Superhighway is not a toll road for the rich." When communication shall be fully privatized as argued earlier, it is expected that rural masses shall face the problem of affording communication. After all to private parties business is business and that is to earn money. Governmental control is required here to see that the common people can afford the communication provided by the private companies.

Environment requires a great deal of attention in any development process. We need to have some ethics[35] for application of technology. "We should not extract or consume resources simply because they are there, or because it is technologically possible to do so, nor should we willfully despoil our environment. In all these respects we should have proper regard for the future consequences of our action." Environment aspect has become a too complicated matter. With increase of GNP, although economy improves but not without pollulating environment. A study[36] reveals that there are three primary areas of environmental scarcity: demand induced scarcity, supply induced scarcity and structural scarcity. Demand induced scarcity occurs when resources are spread more thinly either through population increase or as a result of changes in consumption habits related to economic development. Supply induced scarcity results from the diminution of natural resources caused by either environmental abuse by humans or natural disaster. Structural scarcity "relates to the uneven distribution of resources among population. Population is itself a hazard. Structural scarcity increases with population. Thus, more GNP the more environment hazard. On the other is the hand, to decrease population, UNO has issued a slogan development is the best contraceptive. Let us accept this development a quantity measured by HDI and ICI. Therefore, we can define an environment hazard index (EHI) as:

$$EHI = (GNP + PI) / (HDI + ICI)$$

Accordingly, in Table (2.12), we have shown the position of eight countries in EHI. It is seen that India's position is second. More than EHI worst is the country. The main criminal behind India's worst position is the ICI. If India were average ICI, its position could have gone down to fifth, as shown in Table (2.12). Thus we can decisively say that communication/information infrastructure is the main cause of our poor position in the world context. We have to improve the ICI for which the only path remaining is to fully privatize this sector. Government should not keep it under its control, as it is a high investment and high-risk sector. Along with going for globalization, the developing countries can follow some simple environmental conservation process recently put forward by Mr. William McDonough. These are: (1) waste equals food, (2) current solar income and (3) protection of biodiversity.

It is said, "the Mediterranean was the Ocean of the past, the Atlantic is the Ocean of the present and the Pacific will be the Ocean of the future." India and other developing countries of the Asia-Pacific, if want to be the partner of future Ocean, must go for liberalization in an intelligent and judicious way rather than by haphazard means. A possible effective means for this is illustrated in the paper and pictorially shown in Fig. (2.1).

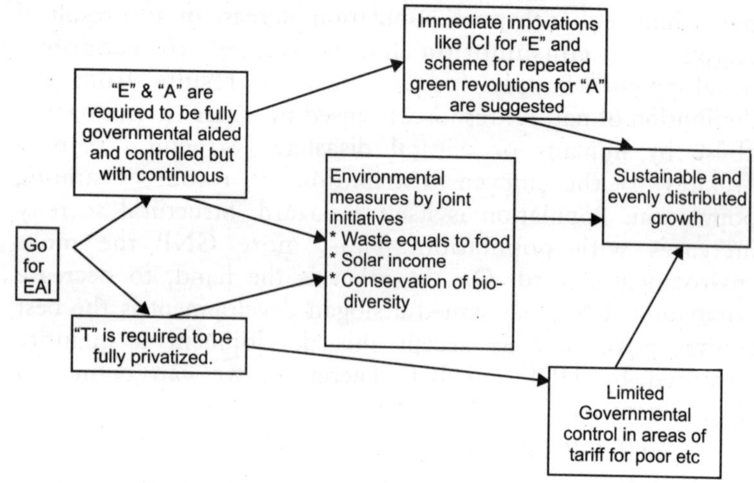

Notes:

E = Education Training and R & D
A = Agriculture
I = Infrasturcture (Communication, information, power, road, railways etc.)

Fig. 2.1: Model for Liberalization for Third World

Table 2.5: GNP (Economic Index)

Country	GNP/Capita in US $ of 1988 (x)	Normalized relative Index (y_1) y_1=x/x max
Japan	20,953	1
Singapore	9,075	0.43
China	326	0.016
India	346	0.017
Thailand	999	0.048
Philippines	642	0.030
France	16,196	0.77
USA	19,819	0.95

Average y_1= 0.41

Table 2.6: PI (Population Index)

Country	Population in millions of 1998 (x)	Normalized relative Index(y_2) y_2= x/x max
Japan	123	0.010
Singapore	2.6	0.002
China	1,178 (1993)	1
India	800	0.679
Thailand	55	0.046
Philippines	59	0.050
France	56	0.047
USA	246	0.209

Average y_2= 0.26

Table 2.7: HDI (Human Development Index)

Country	%GNP in health of 1986 (x_1)	Normalized x_1	%GNP in education of 1986 (x_2)	Normalized x_2
Japan	4.90	0.74	5.00	0.85
Singapore	1.20	0.18	5.20	0.88
China	1.4	0.21	2.70	0.46
India	0.90	0.14	3.40	0.58
Thailand	1.30	0.20	4.10	0.69
Philippines	0.70	0.10	1.70	0.29
France	6.6	1.00	5.9	1.00
USA	4.5	0.68	5.3	0.90

Country	Scientists & Engineers / million population of 1986 (x_3)	Normalized x_3	Average of x_1,x_2 and x_3 (x)	Normalized Relative index y_3= x/x max
Japan	5029	1.00	0.86	1.00
Singapore	1287	0.26	0.44	0.5
China	100	0.02	0.23	0.27
India	109	0.02	0.25	0.29
Thailand	210	0.04	0.31	0.36
Philippines	90	0.02	0.14	0.16
France	1,973	0.04	0.80	0.93
USA	3,317	0.66	0.75	0.87

Average y_3= 0.55

Table 2.8: ICI (Information Consumption Index)

Country	TV sets/100 People (x_1)	PCs per 100 People (x_2)	Phone lines / 100 People (x_3)
Japan	64.1	12	48
Singapore	38	15.3	47.3
China	23.1	0.2	2.3
India	5.5	0.1	1.1
Thailand	18.7	1.2	4.7
Philippines	12.1	0.6	1.7
France	58	14	54.7
USA	79	29.7	60.2

Table 2.9: ICI (Information Consumption Index)

Country	CATV subscribers / 100 people (x_4)	x = Average of x_1,x_2 and x_3	Y_4=x/x max. Normalized relative index
Japan	8.3	33.1	0.69
Singapore	-	33.55	0.698
China	2.5	7.02	0.146
India	1.1	1.95	0.040
Thailand	-	6.15	0.128
Philippines	0.5	3.73	0.077
France	2.8	32.38	0.674
USA	23.2	48.02	1.00

(figures are of 1994) Average y_4= 0.431

Table 2.10: Comparison of Indexes of Economy, Population, Human Development and Information Consumption

Position	Economy	Population	Human Development	Information Consumption
1	Japan	China*	Japan	USA
2	USA	India*	France	Singapore
3	France	USA	USA	Japan
4	Singapore	Philippines	Singapore	France
5	Thailand	France	*Thailand	China*
6	*Philippines	*Thailand	*India	Thailand*
7	India*	Japan	China	Philippines*
8	China*	Singapore	Philippines*	India*

Note:*Countries which are below the average of EI, HDI and ICI; and above the average of PI

Table 2.11: Total Development Index to Population Index Ratio

Country	Average of EI, HDI and ICI (=TDI)	TDI/PI = Signal to noise ratio
Japan	0.896	896
Singapore	0.546	298
China	0.328	0.328
India	0.116	0.170
Thailand	0.179	3.891
Philippines	0.089	07.8
France	0.791	16.829
USA	0.94	4.497

Table 2.12: Environmental Hazard Index

Country	$y_1 + y_2$	$y_3 + y_4$	EHI=$(y_1+y_2)/(y_3+y_4)$	EHI with average y_3 for all countries
Japan	1.010	1.69	0.598	2.34
Singapore	0.432	1.208	0.358	1.00
China	1.016	0.416	2.442	2.35
India	0.696	0.33	2.109	1.62
Thailand	0.094	0.488	0.193	0.22
Philippines	0.080	0.238	0.336	0.18
France	0.817	1.604	0.509	1.90
USA	1.159	1.87	0.620	2.69

Note: In calculations of ICI, HDI, PI and EHI, data of some nearby years have been mixed in very few cases. This will not hamper the arguments derived, and this may cause maximum 5% error.

B: Present analysis

The position of the developing countries in terms of use and application of Information Technology compared to that in developed countries is shown in Tables (2.13-2.15) and in Fig. (2.2). In Table (2.16) the percentage share of information technology for America, Europe and Asia, and that of the e-commerce buyers are shown. It is noticed that in both terms, the position of Asia is very poor. Comparatively, e-commerce is poorer. The picture is illustrated in Fig. (2.2).

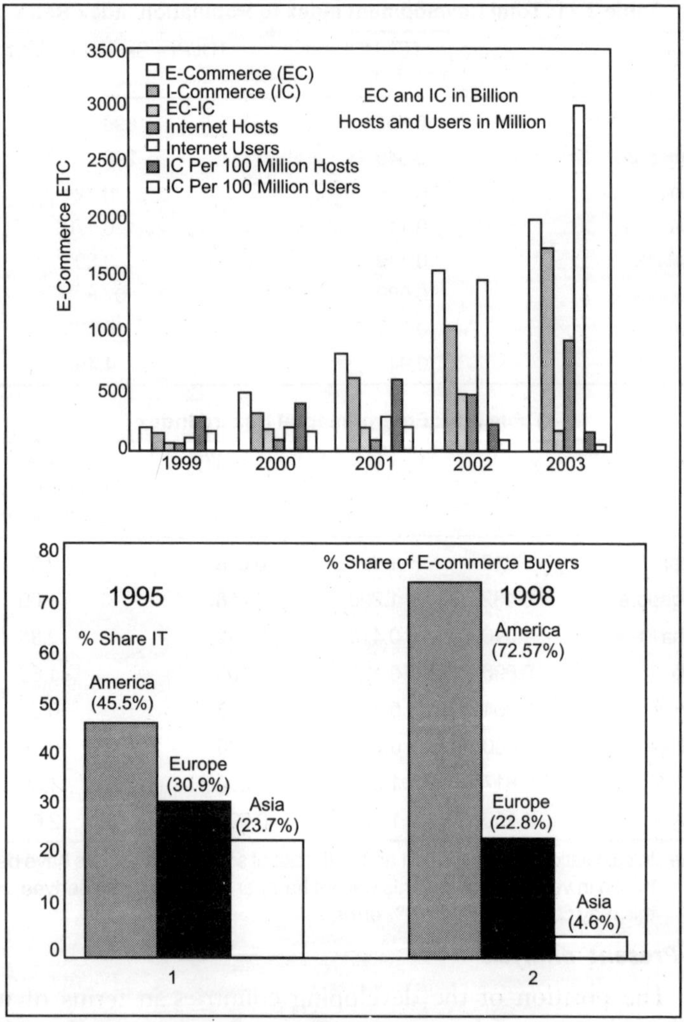

Fig. 2.2: E-Commerce: A World Picture

From these, it is very clear that IT as a technology has become an engine of great inequality. Therefore, the developing countries have to take some bold but strategic initiatives to remove the inequality as because the winners never will try to meet the gap. Many scientists and philosophers in analyzing

Table 2.13 (A): Current Position of Multimedia Tools in Top Ten in the World and India (per 100 people in 1994)

TV Sets		PCs		Phone lines		CATV Subscription	
79	USA	29.7	(USA)	68.3	(Sweden)	37.5	(Netherland)
65	Canada	28.8	(Switzerland)	60.4	(Denmark)	35.7	(Belgium)
64.1	Japan	21.7	(Australia)	60.2	(USA)	32.3	(Switzerland)
58	France	19.3	(Denmark)	59.7	(Switzerland)	26.9	(Canada)
55.1	Germany	17.5	(Canada)	57.5	(Canada)	23.2	(USA)
55	Denmark	17.2	(Sweden)	54.7	(France)	21.9	(Sweden)
49.6	Spain	15.6	(Netherlands)	54	(Hongkong)	18	(Germany)
48.2	Australia	15.3	(Singapore)	50.9	(Netherland)	14.1	(Korea)
48	Sweden	15.1	(UK)	49.6	(Australia)	13.3	(Israel)
48	Aus. Neth	14.4	(Germany)	48.8	(UK)	13.2	(Argentina)
5.5	India	0.1	(India)	1.1	(India)	1.1	(India)

Source: Trudy[22]

Table 2.13 (B): IT Production of Countries

Name of the Country	IT production ($ million)' 90-91
China	892
Hong Kong	2,928
India	952
Japan	44,683
Singapore	6,380
South Korea	3,409
Taiwan	6,149
Indonesia	—
Malaysia	1,315
Thailand	1,190
Mid Value	2,928

Countries below mid value China, India, Malaysia, Thailand

Table 2.14: Main Lines per 100 Inhabitants

Name of the Country	1984	1994	2000
USA	47	64.5	68.7
Canada	45	56	67
Martinique	20	39	56.3
Puerto Rico	18	35	56.3
Guadeloupe	7	36	53.2
Barbados	21	33	40.2
S. Lucia	5	16	39.6
Bahamas	15	29	37.8
Uruguay	8	17	32.7
St. Vincent	4	14	31.5
Belize	4	13	26.5
Trinidad	7	15	25.8

(*Contd...*)

Table 2.14

Name of the Country	1984	1994	2000
Chile	4	11	25.5
Jamaica	3	10	24.6
Argentina	8	15	20.4
Dom. Rep.	2	7	20.1
Suriname	5	11	18.3
Costa Rica	10	14	18
Mexico	5	9	16.6
Colombia	5.5	9.3	16.2
Venezuela	7	10	15.6
Guyana	2	5	14.2
Panama	6.5	10.5	13.9
Brazil	5	7.5	11.6
El Salvador	3	5	8.8
Equador	4	5	8.7
Peru	2.5	3.5	4.7
Paraguay	2.5	3.3	4.3
Bolivia	3	3.4	4
Honduras	1.1	2.5	3.7
Guatemala	2	2.8	3.6
Nicaagua	2	2.4	3.2
Cuba	2.5	3	-
Haiti	.3	.7	-

Table 2.15: IT Production of Countries

Name of the Country	GNP per person in US$ in 1994	% penetration digital/analog cellular in January 1996	Internet users in thousands (1997)	TV sets per 100 people (1994)	PCs per 100 people (1994)	Phone lines per 100 people (1994)	CATV subscribers per 100 people (1994)	IT production ($ million)
Australia	18885	18.10	-	48.2	21.7	49.6	-	-
China	260	0.31	200	23.1	0.2	2.3	2.5	892
Hong Kong	12981	11.82	423	35.9	11.3	54	0.6	2928
India	300	0.01	60	5.5	0.1	1.1	1.1	952
Japan	24290	6.48	3500	64.1	12.0	48.0	8.3	44683
Singapore	11522	10.31	495	38.0	15.3	47.3	-	6380
South Korea	5928	3.76	525	32.4	11.2	39.7	5.8	3409
Taiwan	8816	3.88	480	31.5	8.1	40.0	14.1	6149
Indonesia	598	0.12	100	8.7	0.3	1.3	-	-
Malaysia	3226	5.54	495	23.1	3.3	14.7	-	1315
Thailand	1470	2.13	100	18.7	1.2	4.7	-	1190
Mid-value	5928	3.88	480	31.5	8.1	39.7	5.8	2928
Country below mid value	China India Indonesia Malaysia Thailand	China India South Korea Indonesia Thailand	China Hong Kong India Thailand Indonesia	China India Indonesia Malaysia Thailand	China India Indonesia Malaysia Thailand	China India Indonesia Malaysia Thailand	China Hong Kong India	China India Malaysia Thailand

this, have advocated for improved and skilfull resources generation as the sound strategy for the developing countries. But the irony is that the developing countries under the theme of globalization are in practice of reducing budget for higher education and social sectors. A Nobel Laureate said, "we can not predict the future but we can prepare it." This is what is being done at the developed countries. We in developing countries love to predict rather than to take corrective steps to prepare for the future. Can we change it in the era of KM? If so, how?

The conclusion, therefore from above stated facts and figures is:

That the technology is an engine of great inequality whereas education can meet the gap. The developing countries need to go for education, higher education and research.

Table 2.16: Percentage Share of IT and E-commerce Buyers

	% share of information technology in 1995	% share of E-commerce buyers in 1998
America	45.5	72.57
Europe	30.9	22.8
Asia and Pacific	23.7	4.6

Notes

1. Gerardo R. Ungson and John D. Trudel, "The Emerging Knowledge-based Economy", *IEEE Spectrum*, May, 1999, pp. 60-65.
2. Rekha Prasad, "Technology Import—the Important Issues", *Indian Management, Bombay*, Vol. 36, No. 10, Oct. 97, pp. 36-41.
3. Bhaskar Dutta, "Millenial Dream of Growth", *The Telegraph*, 18 Jan. 2000.
4. A report, *Foreign Affairs*, Sept./Oct. 1997, ICTP Library, Italy.
5. C.T. Bhunia, "Higher Education – Restructuring and Productivity", *University News*, New Delhi, Vol. 38, No. 1, Jan. 2000, pp. 1-4.
6. Bhaskar Dutta, "Millenial Dram of Growth", *The Telegraph*, 18 Jan. 2000.
7. Yoneji Masuda, "Parameters of the Post-industrial Society", *Introduction to Information Technology*, p. 620, Basil Blackwell, U.K., 1985.
8. Rada, "Areas of Impact in IT", p. 517 in Yoenji Masuda, Introduction to Information Technology, Basil Blackwell, U.K., 1985.

9. C.T. Bhunia, Institute-cum-Industry—An Instrument of Survival of Developing Nations, Workshop on Institute Industry Interaction, 19.2.2000, Haldia Institute of Technology.
10. Schumpeter in C. Rangarajan, "Science, Technology and Economic Growth", *Technorama*, IE(I), Calcutta, August, 1999, pp. 25-30.
11. Ela Dutt, "Health Education must for Liberalization Success", *The Statesman*, 24.5.95, p. 20.
12. M. Abdus Salam, Science, Technology and Science Education in the Development of the South, 1991, The Third World Academy of Science.
13. A. Basu, "Education for 21st century", *University News*, Nov.'95, pp. 5-6.
14. R. Narasimhan, "Recounting the Myths and Reality", *The Computer's Today*, March, 1992.
15. C.T. Bhunia et al., A Model Structure of ICI of Electronics and Computer Engineering, ISTE National Seminar-cum-Workshop on Management of Technical Education, Feb. 14-15, 1995, MACT, Bhopal, pp. 1-7.
16. C.T. Bhunia, Institute-cum-Industry — A New Model of Technical Education, *University News*, August, 29, 1994, pp. 11-14.
17. C.T. Bhunia, "Personal Power Development Why and How", *CSI Communications*, March 1996, pp. 7-11.
18. C.T. Bhunia et al., "ICI Revisited", *University News*, Nov. 1995, pp. 1-4, 10.
19. *NERIST Project report* on Government of India, 1984.
20. Edouard Balladur, "At The Crossroads", *The Statesman*, 3.3.97.
21. M. Abdus Salam, Science, Technology and Science Education in the Development of the South, 1991, The Third World Academy of Science.
22. Trudy E. Bell et al., Communications, *IEEE Spectrum*, Jan. '96, pp. 30-41.
23. Kenneth L. Kraemer et al., "From Nationalism to Pragmatism": IT Policy in China, *IEEE Computer Magazine*, August 1995, pp. 64-73.
24. Aileen A. Pisciotta, "Telecommunications Reforms: Options Models and Global Challenges", *IEEE Communication Magazine*, Nov. 94, pp. 28-33.
25. C.T. Bhunia, "ATM Deployment of India", *ITU Conference Asia Telecom* '97, Singapore, 4-9 June '97.
26. Robert R. Bruce, "Restructuring the Telecom Sector in Developing Countries: New Options for Policy Makers", *IEEE Technology and Society Magazine*, Dec. '89, pp. 16-20.

27. James B. Cowie, "Entering the Information Age: Implications for Developing Countries", *IEEE Technology and Society Magazine*, Dec. '89, pp. 21-24.
28. *Maitland Commission Report*, ITU, Geneva, 1984.
29. *Macbridge Commission Report* of World Bank.
30. Ela Dutt, "Health Education must for Liberalization Success", *The Statesman*, 24.5.95, p. 20.
31. Bjorn Wellenius, "The Impact of Modern Telecommunications", *IEEE Technology and Society Magazine*, Dec. 1989, pp. 3-5.
32. Keiji Tachikawa, "Large Scale Urban Disasters and Telecommunications Network", *IEEE Region 10 Asia Pacific Channel*, p. 5.
33. Heather E. Hudson, "Overcoming the Barriers of Distance: Telecommunications and Rural Development", *IEEE Technology and Society Magazine*, Dec. '89, pp. 7-10.
34. Fred T. Hofstetter, *Multimedia Literacy*, McGraw Hill, 1994, p. 157.
35. Anthony E. Gascoigne, "Technology and Ethics", *IEEE Asia-Pacific*, Feb. '96, p. 2.
36. Phillip Howard, "War Over Thinning Pastures", *The Statesman*, 1.3.97.

References

B.P. Lalhi, *Digital Communication System*, Wiley Eastern Ltd.

C.T. Bhunia, "Information Technology in Human Resources Development", *Personal Today*, Jan-March, 1998, pp. 43-47.

D. Carlson, *Communication System*, McGraw Hill.

John Halton, "*The Anatomy of Computing*", *Introduction to Information Technology*, pp. 3-26, Basil Blackwell, U.K., 1985.

Lane Wagger, "Transcendectal Meditation", *Indian Management*, March, 1997.

Stephen Hawking, *Life in Universe* (Lucasian Professor of Mathematics of the University of Cambridge).

Taub and Schilling, *Introduction to Communication Theory*, McGraw Hill.

Wilfred Gappmair Claude E. Shannon, "50th Anniversary of Information Theory", *IEEE Communication Magazine*, April, 1999, pp. 102–105.

Yaswant Deva, "Information Infrastructure", *JIETE Tech Review*, Nov.-Dec., 1996.

3

How to Develop Improved Human Resources in the Developing Countries: Theory of ICI and Studies Thereof

3.1 ICI THEORY

We propose a new model for Technical Education in the name and style of ICI.

The existing technological gap between the developing and the developed countries is high. For example, India is lagging behind 2 to 10 years in technology and by 1 to 10 years in design in reference to international standards. India is one of the countries having poorest per capita consumption of informatics and computers in the world. To catch up with the developed world, the developing countries shall have to invest huge amounts in research and development. And this, the developing countries can hardly afford. Nearly 80% of the vast population, of about 830 million of India is living under poverty line. In such circumstances, how can a developing country like India go for more investment in research and development for high technology and education?

On the other hand, economic, social and the all-round development of any country has become related to utilization of high technology. This we have conclusively studied in section 1 & 2. The war cry for sovereign independence is perhaps over in history. Now is a age for a fight for technological freedom. The third wave has invaded all spheres of our life. The miracle machine of information technology, the computer, is now to play a vital role for the development of science and technology and in promotion of industry, agriculture, economy and social reforms. Today, any national lag is mainly attributed to "not adequately informed" of EC – energy, computer, communication and control. There is, thus, no scope of avoiding high technology.

High technology is a must. For these, huge investment is also a must. But developing countries can't afford the investment. How to solve this puzzle?

One solution often put forward by some developed countries is that the developing countries should not go for high technology rather they can borrow. Many scientists and engineers of the developing countries also share this view on the ground that new high-tech has hardly any market pull in the developing countries. Perhaps they are forgetting the lesson of the history of high-tech utilization. None of the technological developments originated due to customers' pull. Rather, all developments were due to technological push. Thereafter "the advertisements which make the people buy/use things they do not need" create customers' pull. Customers can't come out of this pull due to inherent limits of inertia and lethargy.

At this juncture, we can recall some of the thoughts of Prof. Abdus Salam, Nobel Laureate, on science and technology in developing countries.

Prof. Salam observed that "...creation, mastery and utilization of modern science and technology is basically what distinguished the South from the North...nothing else... neither differing systems of economies, nor of governance, nor differing cultural modes, nor differing perceptions of religious thoughts."

He further observed that "...if there is one lesson to be drawn from the second Gulf air between Iraq and the allies, it is this: no amount of borrowed technology can compete with genuine home grown high technology."

He also said "...the science and technology gap between the south and the North is of relatively recent origin.... Science and Technology are cyclical."

The perception and the thoughts of Prof. Salam are based on proven logic, and therefore beyond question. Hence, the development of high technology must be taken up by developing countries not only for their own sake, but also for the whole of the world.

The answer to the puzzle is therefore clear. The developing countries have to go in for high technology but certainly not in a conventional way, but following the famous Prof's model: "Innovate and Flourish."

And "this is only possible if our people power is superior in terms of knowledge, know-how and innovative capacity. We have already seen that arguments based on the availability of highly qualified but cheap labour are untenable."

To generate excellent people power, the developing countries must restructure the Technological Education Establishment. This paper seeks to propose a new system of technical education.

New Educational Establishment

Problems: The proposed restructured technological educational establishment has to address the few major tasks:

- to remove the obstacles in the way of excellent people power generation in conventional engineering institutes,
- to resource/revenue generation for self-development and achieving excellency with self-independence, and
- to have a structure so that huge investment required for R&D could be generated internally rather than looking to governments.

The first component of tasks was studied in India by many education commissions. It was felt that Indian conventional technological system was not fit: (i) to produce "Technical Engineers"; it produced only "Academic Engineers", and (ii) to attract bright students into the faculty of the institutes, thereby causing brain drain.

Therefore, the problems to be solved by new structural institutes can be listed as:

- production of "Technical Engineers",
- self-revenue generation for investment in R&D, and
- developing measures to attract bright students into faculty.

Modular Structure

A partial solution to the problem was provided by Prof. P.R. Sengupta, who was awarded a German Grand Prize for his contribution on the subject. He for the first time in India executed the project, NERIST (North Eastern Regional Institute of Science & Technology) with a new concept of the modular structure of technical education. According to his concept, 10th class passed students are admitted to the Base-module engineering course. Base module course is equivalent to typical vocational course. Base-module course is of 2 years duration. Top 60% of the Base-module students are allowed to get admission into 2 years higher module known as diploma. Top 60% of diploma-module students are allowed entry to next 2 years degree module. Thus for an entry of 100 students, 40, 36 and 24 students will respectively be Base-level/ vocational engineer, diploma engineer (Technicians) and full-fledged Engineer. Thus, a single institute will be able to provide technical manpower needs at all levels – this indirectly reduces the investment on technical education. Existing conventional education system needs two to three institutes for producing such manpower at different levels.

However, the main objective of producing "Technical Engineers" has been fulfilled here by six and four years continuous exposure to technical fields for degree and diploma holders respectively rather than 4 years and 3 years respectively in conventional system existing in India.

NERIST Project in India is about 20 years old. The analysis of the project reveals that the main goal of the project has been achieved to a large extent. The outgoing NERIST students are seen to be more professional and better trained than those from conventional engineering institutes. But excellence, as desired, is yet to be reached.

Many educational commissions in India have suggested extensive university industry linkage as a remedial measure.

Therefore, to make a success of the NERIST project it should be converted to an ICI (Institute-cum-Industry).

ICI: Institute-Cum-Industry

The solution to the problem of internal generation of resources for investment lies in an innovative educational institute – the Institute-cum-Industry (ICI).

Out of the two department, the role of the industrial department will be to implement. Commercially viable projects in which the final year degree/postgraduate students will be the major and main contributors. The completion of projects in the full last year of respective courses will be mandatory for awarding degree to the students. What is harm if a group of final year degree students of electronics discipline are asked to design a fully commercial PC set as a compulsory part of their degree courses? Is it not possible to ask a group of final year postgraduate students of electronics that the complete design and installation of a packet switched network for a region a mandatory for getting degree?

The industry department will also conduct the practical classes of the degree/postgraduate classes under the supervision of the concerned faculty member of the institute department. The practical classes of the certificate and diploma classes can also be conducted in the industry department. The faculty members may be allowed to do their research work in the industry department with full liberty for which there will be a separate section.

The intake to the proposed ICIs shall comprise 10th passed students as in modular scheme, thereby combining two innovative ideas. However, education structure will be somewhat different from modular scheme as indicated below:

1. 1.5 years will be the duration for certificate course for vertical mobility students. 0.5 year more will be required to be put in by students terminating studies at industry section.
2. 1.5 years will be the duration for diploma course, and only top 60% students of certificate course will be admitted to diploma courses provided they secure more than or equal to certain percentage of aggregate marks in the certificate course. For students terminating their studies at diploma level, 0.5 year

additional industrial training will be in industry section.

3. 3 years will be the duration for degree course and admission procedure will be as in diploma level but based on both the results of certificate and diploma. The specialized course will be offered at the first year of degree course. The special papers will be allotted 50% of aggregate marks of total marks.
4. 1.5 years will be the duration for P.G. course out of which 0.5 year will be for theory class, 0.5 year for project and 0.5 year will be kept reserved for research (extension of project) in respective specialization with the condition that based on this research at least one paper must be published by individual student/group in order to make them eligible for the award of the degree.

In the ICI theory, duration has been fixed for certificate (base)/and diploma courses on the basis of the requirements of "know-how", while for degree and postgraduate courses the duration has been fixed on the basis of the needs of "know-why."

The industry section will earn revenue for running the institute as well as for investment in R&D. By this the developing countries can overcome the financing problem of higher education and research.

Further Seeing into ICI

To be brief, the ICI is:

(1) An innovative type of technical education system that will produce technical engineers rather than academic engineers at different levels.

(2) A cost effective higher education system.

(3) An internal revenue generator (IRG) establishment.

(4) An institute which can flourish industries innovatively and economically.

(5) An institute which can raise status and pay-scale of faculty members.

In the ICI, an environment will have to be created by combined effort of teachers and engineers for students to "LEARN BY DOING" and nor by "studying" in classes only. This will be in line with the spirit of famous PORTER's model of competitive success ....

Factor driven — investment driven – innovation driven.

The current form of industry and institute interaction has many limitations: No common goal, no common initiative, no solid bond for mutual benefits, distrust in interaction, lack of confidence on one another, many constrains, both operational and procedural, ego conflicts in sharing.

In the proposed ICI theory, sharing is solid and complete with single unit operation and single direction. Pictorially the comparison is shown in Figs. (3.1 & 3.2).

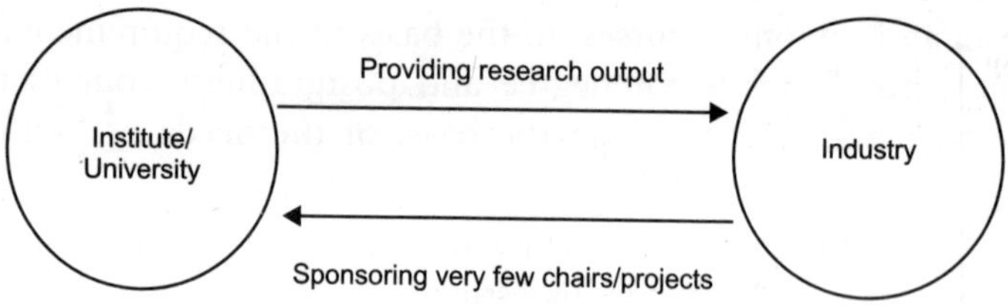

Fig. 3.1: Present Scenario

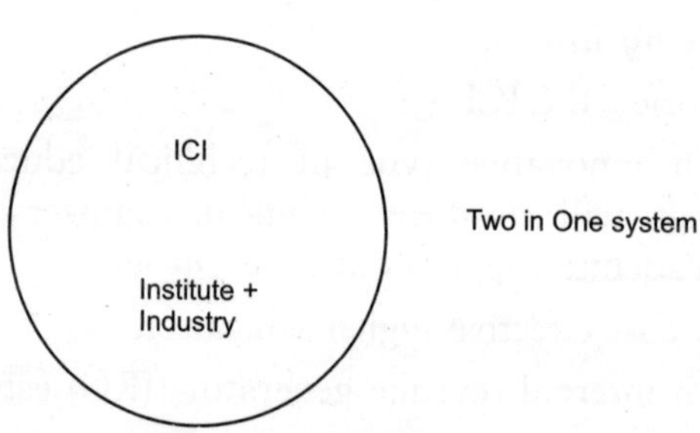

Fig. 3.2: ICI Scenario

QUANTITATIVE COMPARISON

If collaboration is additive:

If in the current model any one unit shares α ($\alpha<1$) part of other potential, the total potential is $N + N.\alpha$ where N is a measure of potential of one unit.

In ICI, the potential is 2N.

For all purposes $2N > (N+N.\alpha)$ ...(1)

If collaboration is multiplicative:

Under the same assumptions used in case of additive collaboration, the potential in current scenario is $N(\alpha.N) = N^2\alpha$.

The ICI provides a potential of N^2. Now for all purposes, $N^2 > N^2\alpha$ .....(2)

From inequalities (1) and (2), it is established that ICI is potentially better system than the current system (Fig. 3.3).

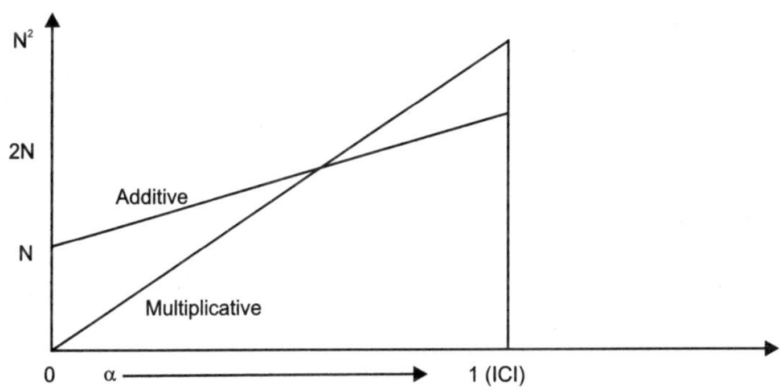

Fig. 3.3: Multiplicative curve is of ICI, Additive curve is of current scenario

Curbing Brain Drain

In order to attract bright students in teaching and research and to curb the brain what is required is that the status and the pay-scale of faculty members in developing countries be increased. In India while just a graduate holding a Central Government gazetted post becomes Director in the pay scale of Rs. 18,400–22,400; a Ph.D/D.Sc. degree holder in a university/

allied teaching service becomes an assistant professor in the same pay scale and with much less perks. This is really humiliation and indeed a negative point of teaching service. Prof. Salam described, "high thinking and plain living" as a hypothetical consideration in today's scenario. We propose an administrative structure of ICI as in Fig. (3.4).

In India, for people-power generation in software of computer engineering, UGC can introduce DCA/MCA courses. It is felt that modular scheme can be implemented here also. Students will be admitted into integrated 3 years MCA course. After first year 60% students based on merit may be dropped with DCA and only top 40% students may be asked to go for MCA degree.

Administering ICIs

An autonomous body whose members will be only the professional persons of concerned discipline will run the institute using modern methods of management based on paperless automated office and where decisions are to be taken instantaneously based on MIS, etc. The examination procedures including selection of paper-setters, examiners and preparation of results will be done by computers only.

Regarding promotion/recruitment policy/procedures, the following innovative steps are suggested:

1. Recruitment will be at lowest root level (Asst. Director and below) and at the level of Deputy Director General and above. The basis of selection will be the candidates' academic qualifications, experience and achievements in terms of publications and allied matters and absolutely not on boss's reports. There will be assigned marks for each of these comments. For this, the universities/institutes and their degrees may be graded. The experience will be graded by the length of service, and publications by quality in reference to journal/conference/magazine. A software may be designed for this purpose to calculate the total grades of a candidate based on these criteria. The selection/promotion will only be based on the grading so determined.

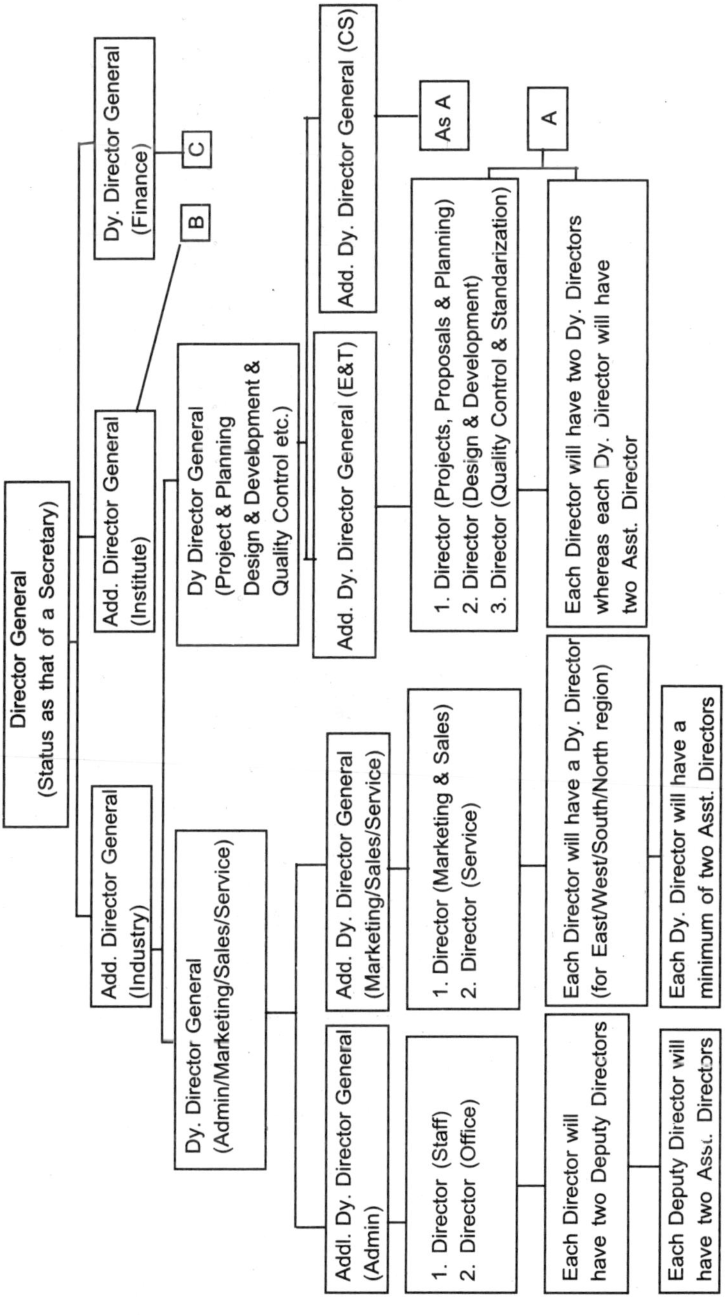
Director General
(Status as that of a Secretary)
Add. Director General
(Industry)
Add. Director General
(Institute)
Dy. Director General
(Finance)
C
B
Dy. Director General
(Admin/Marketing/Sales/Service)
Dy Director General
(Project & Planning
Design & Development &
Quality Control etc.)
Addl. Dy. Director General
(Admin)
Add. Dy. Director General
(Marketing/Sales/Service)
Add. Dy. Director General (E&T)
Add. Dy. Director General (CS)
As A
A
1. Director (Staff)
2. Director (Office)
1. Director (Marketing & Sales)
2. Director (Service)
1. Director (Projects, Proposals & Planning)
2. Director (Design & Development)
3. Director (Quality Control & Standarization)
Each Director will
have two Deputy Directors
Each Director will have a Dy. Director
(for East/West/South/North region)
Each Director will have two Dy. Directors
whereas each Dy. Director will have
two Asst. Director
Each Deputy Director will
have two Asst. Directors
Each Dy. Director will have a
minimum of two Asst. Directors

Fig. 3.4 (A)

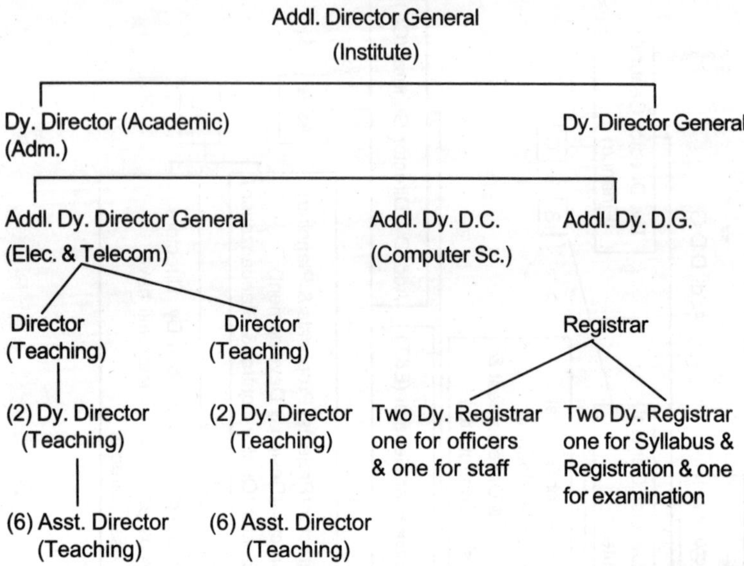

Fig. 3.4 (B)

Dy. Director General
(Finance)

Director Finance (Industry)	Director Finance (Institution)
Suitable Offices	Suitable Office

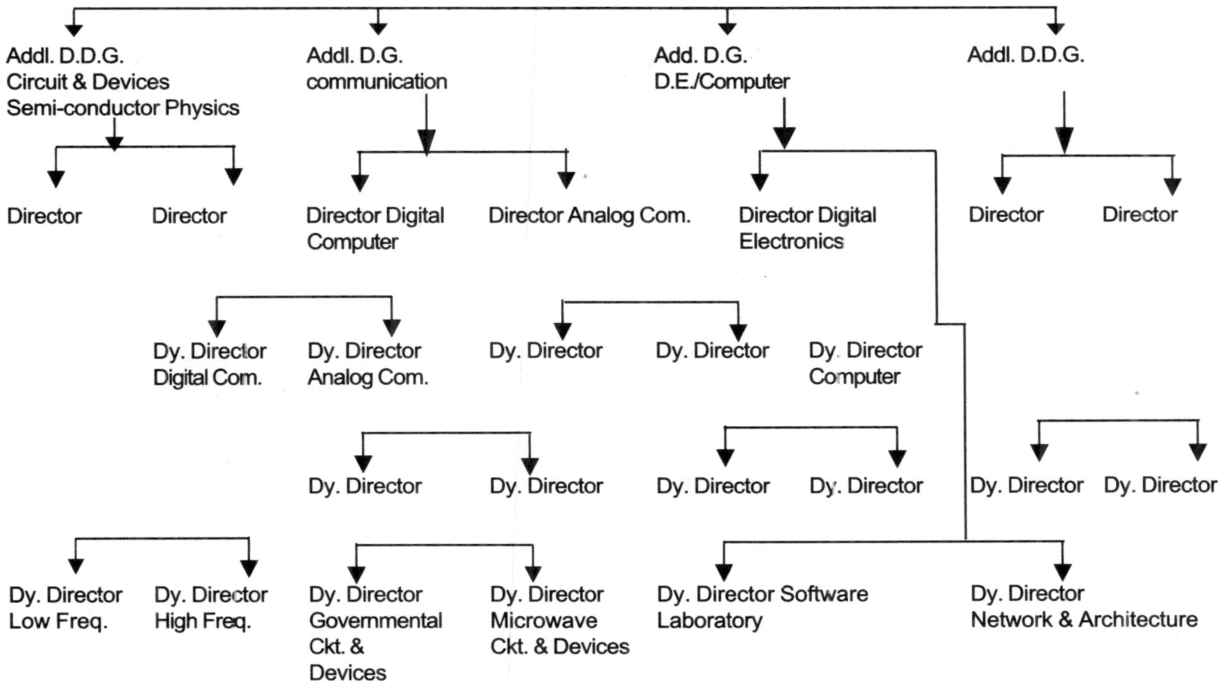

Fig. 3.4(C)

Fig. 3.4: A porposed structure for two deptts.

2. Promotion from the lowest root level maximum up to the Addl. Deputy DG will be internal and based on merit only and will be within the age of 40 years of the candidate. The merit will be graded as above.

The Director General must be from the teaching section. He will be selected on the basis of his ability and grade points. No minimum age need to be prescribed.

The ICI is the solution to the puzzle – need of high-tech vs. investment for high-tech. This needs a trial. This is an attempt to give institutes/universities the corporate status. The objectives behind the new model are: (a) to provide emphasis on production of qualified man power rather than quantitative, (b) to implement concept of total internal revenue generation, (c) to realize practical and fruitful interaction between industry and institute, (d) to implement the concept of modular technical education, and (e) to meet with the existing technology gap between developed world and developing world, etc. The concept is totally based on proven logic and scientific thoughts of renowned scientists like Prof. A. Salam, Prof. U.R. Rao, etc. The ICI concept is filling to the market oriented economy also. Indeed, the NERIST project in India can be converted to such a project.

3.2 REVIEWING ICI IN LIGHT OF "PERSON-POWER DEVELOPMENT: WHY & HOW"

Person-Power Development—Why and How

Computer Society of India has recently come out with a national IT policy. One of the important recommendations of the policy draft is person-power development. There are historical evidences that without human resources development no nation can develop. India cannot just ignore this solid strategy. CSI's recent recommendation is thus worth accepting. But any attempt to improve person-power by conventional and/or copied systems could be counter-productive. We need to have and implement some innovative and environmental friendly system for us. There is growing requirement of contingency management. In light of these aspects, in this article we shall explore some novel ideas for person-power development along with critical review of existing systems.

The world is in the throes of information revolution brought forward by a whole cluster of highly interactive and diffusive technologies like electronics, computer and communication. The development indicators of the countries in the world have become "information rich" and "information poor." The promise the information technology holds for improving ourselves include social, economic, political and industrial developments at national, regional and global level. The impact the information technology causes on development processes is by three major ways of improving: effectiveness (measure of doing right things), efficiency (measure of doing things right) and quality (measure of satisfaction, durability and usage).

It is well understood that information technology is the right tool for developmental activities in agriculture, health, education, political and industrial development is indispensable feature of information technology. For example, farmers can verify the market rates of their produce in different markets by which they can get the highest prices. This will eliminate the middleman business now existing in rural areas of the developing world. The severe dearth of qualified doctors in rural areas is a serious problem in the Third World. The consultancy and advice through information technology can solve the problem. Mass and adult education through satellite communication are well known applications of information technology. The information technology compensates time and distance problem of remote areas. A study of World Bank reveals that benefit to cost ratio in use of telecommunication ranges from 5:1 to 100:1. The human resources development and political liberty can be earned through information technology. UNESCO's MacBride Commission reported that: "There can be no genuine, effective independence without the communication resources needed to safeguard it."

On the industrial and the business sectors, the role of information technology is profound. On business, information technology offers a global competitive advantage. Post and person travel even in sales and marketing are being reduced due to advertisement through electronics. The stronger, more complex but more productive interaction and business are possible. Physical constraints in terms of machinery (automobiles) and men on business are reducing. On industrial sector, just-in-time repairing of faulty plants, delivery of spare and availability of expert opinion without any space and scale constraints make the sector to flourish. 3S (Synergy = Synthesis + Energy, Symbiosis = Synthesis + Biology, and Serendipity = individual universe) management is new management driven by information technology. The 3S management increases productivity.

Culture, Technology and Society

Life on earth has to overcome the crisis for sustaining and creating conditions for survival and existence. Human being has complemented the existence, the growth, the prosperity and the development using technology. Since long back, there has been existing a feeling that the application of technology has an emphasis on the culture and the society.

In this section, the correlation, the reflection and the relation between culture and technology, particularly in the era of liberalization, globalization and privatization era duly brought forward by a single most technology known as Information Technology, have been examined.

Culture consists of values, ideas, language, means of socializing and getting foods, clothes and shelter, customs, codes, art, rituals ceremonies, use of tools, machines and techniques according to Majumdar (1996) so forth. Culture is the means and the ways of living of a given society (While 1959; Russel & Pelto 1972; Claxton 1997; Dunn 1978 and Urevbee, 1997) the definition of culture stipulated at the UNESCO conference held in Mexico in 1982, is "Culture comprises the whole complex of distinctive spiritual, intellectual and emotional features that characterize society or social group. It includes not only arts and letters, but also modes of life, the fundamental rights of the human being, value systems, traditions and beliefs." The second draft adopted in Mexico city proposed, culture as "a complex, comprehensive and multidimensional process which extends beyond mere economic growth, incorporates all dimensions of life and all the energies of a community, all of whose members are called upon to make a contribution and expect to share the benefits. Mode of life is a part of culture. Discoveries and innovations are the essential elements for the life to survive, prosper and grow.

As per contemporary writer Raymond Williams, culture consists of four things: State of habit of mind, state of in intellectual development, general body of arts and the way of material life. With the discovery of light, solely discovered by people through necessity and innovation and discovers are attributes to changing life styles and modes, causing culture to change. Thought process, when early people began to live in groups, is also an essential attribute for change of modes of life. Innovation discovers thoughts and their applications are what we call science, philosophy and technology. Actually belief, science and philosophy are three categories of the intellectual activities of human beings which are essential ingredients of society: "belief where no questions are asked; philosophy, where all questions are asked and debated on the basis of logic; and science, where some questions are ruled out because ... science is what can be tested by experiment and observation. Amartya Sen stated that, "central to culture is freedom; and in particular to value, and what lives we have reason to seek." This culture is the totality of the scientific, technological, philosophical, psychological, ideological and economical features of a given society. With change of any of these, culture is bound to change. Culture is a dynamic system, a system which changes with time and a system which changes, gets evolution with time.

What is technology? It is the application of science. More specifically technology is the application of the various branches of knowledge in general and of science in particular to practical problems. With technology, people solve the problems and master over the environment. Technology is the accumulated practical knowledge, experiences, skills and procedures "for making, using and doing useful things and for accomplishing recognized purposes. Technology includes not only modern industrial technology, i.e., techniques, tools and machines but also crafts the artifacts, what is sometimes referred to as the material culture." Technologies sometimes are defined as material and non-material technology. Material technology refers to all tangible objects like machines, tools and equipment used by people in their environment and activities of solving problems. Non-material technology refers to ideas, thoughts, philosophies, customs and frameworks embodied in social processes. Education, training, economic ideologies, political processes and procedures are classified as non-material technology.

Culture is an envelope of non-material technologies. Non-material technologies are changed and institutionalized by material technology. Thus, "there is a natural inter-dependence between technology and culture which requires that the relationship be an essentially authentic one, since it exits to satisfy man's immediate and particular needs as well as to enable him to live in harmony with his very own environment. Indeed tools are the interface between man and nature. The development of new technologies is linked to a society's evolving needs, to the relative importance accorded to satisfying them, and to the application of new and different solutions to existing practical problems based on the society's creative capacity and its particular knowledge and experiences. The introduction of a new technology often creates new social situation, which in turn, creates new values, thus stimulating further technological development." Culture and technology are interlinked and vary with each other, change with each other and enrich with each other. The implication of Raymond William's definition of culture is that the technology is an element of culture, the depth of change and that of enrichment of the culture. The depth of change and that of enrichment of the culture due to technology adoption in a given society depend on many factors:

1. Educational level.
2. Economical level.
3. Corporate culture.

4. Ethnic, gender and cultural composition.
5. Available Infrastructure, technology and skill.
6. Psychological profile.

However, the basic factors are: (i) Average education (E_1), (ii) Average economic level (E_2), (iii) Political stability and openness (P), (iv) Information flow and availability (I) One can write: Cultural change – f_1 (technology adoption)

Technology adoption [1] $= f_2 (E_1, E_2, P, I)$

Cultural change $= f_3 (E_1, E_2, P, I)$

Cultural change $= f_4$ (GNP/GDP, HRI, P, IR/IP)

It will be pertaining to mention about Amartya Sen's observation (*Encyclopedia Britannica*) that, "Education is important not just for the help that it might give to economic growth, but because it is an essential part of cultural development." The observation that is put in the above four equations can be corroborated by the statistics of international culture in terms of printed materials, cinema, photography, fine and graphic arts, audio-visual field, sporting games and equipment in 1991. This is depicted in Table (3.1).

Table 3.1: Culture Development Scenario

	Share in the world export of the cultural goods	% of world population
Developing nations	68.2%	23%
Developed nations	31.8%	77%

On the information sector, one can verify our observation just on the basis of the number of simple radio receivers per 1000 people (Table 3.2). Arguing on the political nature of technology, Professor Andrew O. Urevba wrote that, "While we admit that technology is cultural enterprise, we must not fail to be aware of the political nature of technology as well."

In the developed world, with applied technology (machines, gadgets, etc.) in all aspects of human life we are dependent on machines and gadgets, not to mention the whole infrastructure of societal living. There is a feeling that the technology has taken over. This line of thought has arisen because of the political nature of technology.

Table 3.2: Number of Radio Receivers

	Number of receivers (Millions)				Number of necessitous Inhabitants				% in terms of world total (number of receivers)			
	1970	1980	1990	1994	1970	1980	1990	1994	1970	1980	1990	1994
World total	771	1307	1877	2008	209	294	335	357	-	-	-	-
Africa	19	49	160	122	51	104	171	173	2.46	3.74	5.75	6.07
America	350	566	711	756	687	926	991	991	45.39	43.3	37.87	37.64
Asia	78	254	568	621	37	96	178	183	10.11	19.43	30.26	30.92
Europe	314	418	464	481	604	643	643	662	40.72	31.98	24.72	23.95
Oceania	10	20	26	28	526	871	996	1007	1.29	1.53	1.38	1.39
Developing Countries	123	323	724	790	46	97	177	179	15.95	21.71	38.57	39.34
Least Developed Countries	7	20	48	55	23	51	95	98	90	1.53	2.55	2.73

Both, the nature of present technology and technological innovation and maintenance are politically determined. In other words, "technology does not just provide in its individual machines the physical means by which a society supports and promotes its power structure, it also reflects as a social institution this social structure in its design." And one finds that education is the basic tool for technology adoption, cultural growth and societal improvements.

Problems and Solutions in Age of IT

Scientific research has conclusively established that man is a part of nature. The technology that is an application of science has since thus following the science that has been now attained to implement animalization of machine and vice versa, the latest manifestation of which is intelligent computer and its predicted applications. While the aim of science is to find answer to "why nature is like as it is" or "what makes nature as it is", the technology apparently speaking or as is told, aims to address the central social issues of reducing poverty and the gap between "haves" and "have nots." But critical looks belie the goals of the technology. Neither the poverty has been eliminated on the mother earth nor the gap between the rich and the poor has been reduced in past ages of industrial technology and in the present age of information technology. At present scenario it is widely unexpected to see any reverse trend in the coming up knowledged society. Where lies the fault in not achieving the goal of technology? Is it in technology itself? Is it the political nature of application of technology? Or is the policy decision of the application of technology the culprit? Before we critically look into the issues, it will be undoubtedly desirable to look into the problem in depth. In the present age of information technology, the problem of disparity has been given a technical name called "Digital Divide", that defines the division of the society into parts of information and access to information "haves" and "have nots." In general all the developed countries belong to "Information Rich" and the rest of the world to "Information Poor." In such a scenario, what strategy the developing countries should follow to lead into the "knowledge age?" Therefore, a new solution in our form, I call Indian Solution, for a solid collaboration is the need of the hour. In this context, the concept of "ICI" (Institute-cum-Industry) is a powerful solution. While these problems are duly addressed in several other studies[1-3], the studies of applying IT in general and networking in particular for improving the higher technical education is yet to be made in perspective of developing countries.

The role of information technology on social aspects and particularly in well-being of family is exciting. The service of information technology for contacting with kin, friends and relatives and preserving our life, health and property is well known.

Seen from the viewpoint of Kenichi Ohmae's "triad power" comprising North America, Western Europe, and Japan, it is anybody's guess that information revolution will lead their societies to more and more advanced, sophisticated and developed stage. How does the prospect of information technology fit into Third World? What will be the effect of this emerging technology on the developing economy in near future? In our world, three-fourths of total population live in the developing countries. All the developing countries together consume one-eight of world's total output. So although, enthusiasm and optimism are there, the picture of adoption of information technology in Third World is not yet clear.

The major problem is that most of the IT is being borrowed. This causes a huge flow of money from developing countries to developed countries. Will the Third World be able to afford it? Technology is moving fast. Within a span of just 50 years we have seen not less than 4 generations of computer systems. Since 1980s, molecular electronics has been augmented.

This may pose a threat to conventional electronics technology. The concept of chemical computing may replace the conventional electronics computing. Today's research and development take no time in between laboratory development and commercial product. This is due to techno-economic hectic competition in the developed countries. The rapidity with which IT is flourishing is beyond imagination. For example, switching speed of today's transistor is 1 billion times as fast as those of 50 years ago. See that today's ultrasonic planes move only 100 times as fast as horse drawn cartridge. The so fast rapidity of IT and no time gap in between laboratory development and commercial produce have made the life period of IT related industrial products a bare minimal. How then developing countries should cope with borrowing under such rapid changing environment? Today's imported things become outdated tomorrow.

To this problem, there has been added one more new problem. Before 1970s, raw materials were used to be exported from Third World to the developed world and finished products were used to be imported into Third World from the developed world. This was a near balanced world business. But with new techniques in hand, developed countries are increasing the substitutions of raw materials since 1970s. As such world business has gradually become unidirectional.

Therefore, how do the developing countries fit into this picture? If a sound and suitable development strategy is not adopted, the outright application of IT in the Third World will further deteriorate world balance. By judicious selection and intelligent application of IT, the Third World could manage the gap. For example, developing countries must give priority of using IT in family planning, mass education and development of agricultural sectors. Another development strategy shall be to raise HRD (Human Resources Development). Prof. Colombo, a famous Italian Scientist pointed out that "the most important resource in today's world is human intelligence, creativity and ingenuity. Education and training must be number one priority in any development process."

Very recently Computer Society of India (CSI) has published reports of INTENT (Information Technology for National Transformation). Three broad areas of recommendations of INTENT are:

- Promoting IT applications

- Improving the IT infrastructure
- Person-power development

Person-power development or HRD is one of these recommendations, although it has got the third position. I think HRD deserves the first position and there is a historical proof that without HRD nothing can develop. Owen, the first management guru in the world, raised his industry to a flourishing stage by improving "Virtual Machines", the term he used for people of his industry. In the article we shall critically analyze all the aspects of person-power development pertaining to higher education.

Problems of Higher Education

Higher education is an important means of person-power development particularly for IT and its growth in any country. But it is a common feeling that higher education is quite expensive in India, and in developing countries in general. In recent days the gravity of this feeling has augmented. It was even reported that synergy committees, formed by MHRD of Government of India, to reevaluate the different education systems in India have recommended to divert the expenditure of higher education towards basic education. Of course, basic education is an essential element for overall prosperity and growth of any country. Therefore, it is justified to allocate more funds on basic education. But it is not understood why at the cost of higher education. Actually, educational expenditure at different levels in Third World is really meager compared to developed countries. One can have a look at Table (3.3)[4,5] for comparison.

It is neither justified to cut the budget of higher education nor to limit growth of higher education. It will be a good exercise to examine the reasons of expensiveness of higher education of India and thereby taking appropriate measures to curb the same.

The present system of higher education is expensive in India because of several reasons out of which important reasons are:

1. The lack of integrated approach in the education system.
2. The brain drain which denies investment returns.
3. The lack of political and Government, will to utilize the products of higher education.
4. The prejudice and the preference towards some institutes in allocation of budgets, etc.

However, this is the time when we must address these problems rather than limiting higher education in any aspect.

Why Higher Education

Higher education is a must for mere survival in this age of competition, a report published in *IEEE Spectrum*[6] showed that Ph.D.s are more innovative than managers, scientists and engineers at bachelor's and master's level. Porter's model of success is "Innovate or Perish." It is therefore a simple logical extension that higher education is a must for any development process.

How to Solve the Problems of Higher Education

Problems (1) and (2) as listed earlier can be solved to a large extent by restructuring higher education in the form of ICI (Institute-Cum-Industry). ICI is a well-established theory[7-9].

We often claim that India is the third largest country in the world in technical man-power. But to this claim, there remain two fallacies. In India number of educated people has increased with increase in population, but certainly technical institutes have not increased in same proportion. About 80% educated people are of general education. This has caused a stiff competitiveness in admission to engineering and medical colleges. Many private coaching institutes and tutors earn huge money by imparting coaching for admission tests basically to the child of elite society who can only pay sky-rise fees of these coaching institutes and tutors. Essentially by this, meritorious students particularly those who are economically backward are being deprived of chances of admission in technical institutes. Next, there has been a growing feeling that our present technical institutes are not producing the needed technical human resources to achieve rapid industrial growth to compete with world market. It is often said that present system of technical education in general has failed to produce "technical engineers".

India, therefore, requires to set up more technical institutes on one hand, whereas it also needs to restructure its technical institutes to address the existing drawbacks. At the same time it has been observed that solely state financing of high education and research is not justified and affordable to. However, the present system of technical education in India copied system of Western countries. This goes against the principle of present days' contingency management theory which is based on management by circumstances. We could set up ICI to produce better skilled manpower, to realize internal revenue generation (IRG) scheme in institutes and to curb brain drain.

Survey on ICI

Recently a survey was conducted to see the acceptability of the ICI proposal. Response was received from Directors/Professors/Readers/Lecturers/Students. The result of survey is portrayed in Fig. (3.5). It is seen that:

- Over all, ICI has been preferred to the existing structure of education system.
- Younger generation prefers ICI more than older generation.

Therefore ICI needs experiment in India.

The general survey on technical education in India gives a similar picture. From a survey on problems and prospects of higher education in India conducted by the authors, a few interesting findings are given below:

1. To a question of the nature of problem being faced by the scientists, the response received is as below:

Financial	42%
Scientific	30%

Administrative	42%
Non-availability of materials	15%

2. To a question of whether Research and Development (R&D) be given special priority 100 per cent response goes in its favour. ICI supports this response.
3. To a question of industry and institute interaction in the field of R&D, more than 50 per cent say about its extreme essentiality ICI is a 100 per cent interaction scheme.
4. To a question of growth of indigenous research, 100 per cent responses go in its favour. ICI can augment indigenous research.
5. To the requirements of development of Science and Technology, responses received are as under:

Higher salary and perks	42%
Placing scientists and engineers at top positions of technical departmentts/sections	70%
Substantial budget provision in R&D and higher education	100%

ICI can conform with such requirements.

6. To a question of priority areas of research and development, responses received are as below:

Information Technology	14%
Power Sector	28%
Electronics and Communication	28%
Environmental studies	14%
Biological Science and Human Science	14%

Based on this, we establish ICI as acceptable and appropriate model for technical education in the changed scenario.

Problem (3) as enumerated earlier is quite serious in nature. Today theory of TQM (Total Quality Management) defines that students are products rather than customers. It was recently elaborated in an article in ISTE news by Dr. S. Mullick, Principal, TTTI, Calcutta. For returns on investment, products should be properly utilized. Dr. S. Basu in one of his articles[10] observed that even in "project specific matters" in government, "authority rests with the bureaucracy." Therefore, professionalism, inventions and innovations are on declining trend. The net result is the import of technologies and techniques. A result of survey on who is best suited to be Vice Chancellor/Director is shown in (Fig. 3.2).

Government and political leaders should have to rethink over the issue. They should realize the changing requirement of professional and management skills (Fig. 3.3) in all spheres of our life because of the use of more machines and automation everywhere.

Regarding last problem, we should note that none of Sir J.C. Bose, Acharya P.C. Roy, S.N. Bose, Meghnad Saha, Homi Bhabha, C.V. Raman among others was a product of any today's preferred institute of any kind. It is people who should be chosen rather than particular institute or organization for allocation of funds for research and development. Our prolonged exercise and experiments in the fashion of giving priority by prejudice and preference have proven to be marginal success only.

We also note that "Talent is colour blind. Talent is gender blind. Talent has nothing to do with dialects, whether they're Hispanic or Irish or Polish or Chinese."[11]

Conclusion

For people-power, higher education is a must. It is not expensive on innovation and redefined forms. Nation today badly needs higher education in a modified fashion. For growth and fruitful application of IT we need that type of people-power which may be products of ICI. One solution of INTENT's recommendation of person-power development could be ICI by its rights only. ICI will by its right give a solution of the century old problem that Bill Ratterec, member of Secretaries of ILO[12] said: "As far as salaries and other material benefits are concerned, the evidence suggests that with a few exceptions in high income countries, teachers' salaries have been low."

In ancient times, knowledge was taken as power. With industrial age, technology took away the power from knowledge. But with the third wave and the consequent all-round impacts of information technology (IT) on society and economy, the power is back to basic. Today knowledge is power. Knowledge has become saleable. It has now been recognized all over world that the most previous resource is the human resource, the resource of knowledge and the resource of over fertilizer brain. For developmental and economic advantages, human resource development (HRD) has been recognized as the most important tool in this age of information. Peter Drucher Bill opined that, "the leading original group of the knowledge society shall be knowledge workers and knowledge executives who know how to allocate knowledge to productive use ..... Yet, unlike the employees under capitalism, they will own both, the means of production and the tools of production ..... The crucial point about a post-industrial society is that knowledge and information become the strategic and transforming resources of the society, just as capital and labor have been the strategic and transforming resources of the industrial society." As per the report[13] "education seems more closely tied than ever to an individual's economic success, according to a 1996 study by Frank Leavy, Professor of urban economics at the Massachusetts Institute of Technology (MIT), in Cambridge. He found that 15 years ago a typical college graduate took home 38 per cent more than worker with a high school diploma, whereas today, a typical college educated worker takes in 73 per cent more. Arthur Lewis observed that, "The central problem in the theory of economic development is to understand the process by which a community which was previously saving and investing 4% or 5% of its national income or less, converts itself to an economy where voluntary saving is running at about 12% to 15% of national income or more. This is the main problem because the central fact of economic development is rapid capital accumulation (including knowledge and skill with capital)."

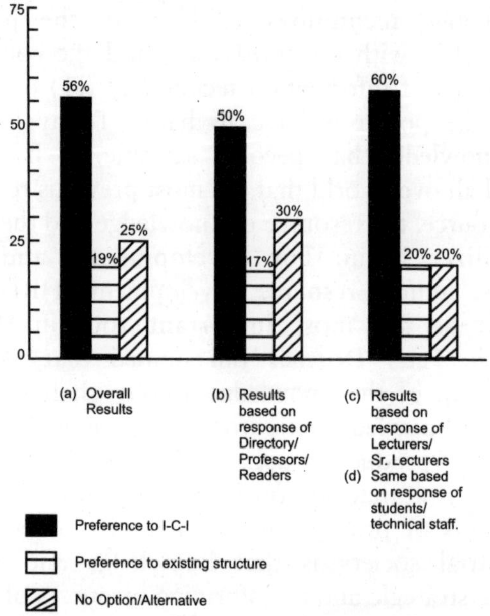

Fig. 3.5: Younger generation give more preference to ICI.

In 1979, a 30 year old man with a high school diploma earned a yearly average US$ 27,000 dollars (in USA) whereas by 1993, his salary had drowned down US $ 20,000. According to the statistics from the Census Bureau, earnings (in constant dollars) of college graduates grew slightly over the same period.

The advantages in computers and other technologies, as well as the demands of competition in the international marketplace, are swiftly transferring the skills used in factories, healthcare, food processing, construction, energy production, banking insurance, and many other occupations. Even the lowest jobs required some mathematics and science skills. No one has articulated this insight better than MIT economics professor Lester Thruow, who in an article in the *Sunday New York Times* of 16 February 1997 was quoted as stating, "Those with Third World skills will earn Third World wages".

Besides, our education system and structure are all copied from the developed nations, and therefore there is a wide uncover able mismatch between what we need and what we are doing in education sectors. This is why we often feel our higher education is costly, and this is why we fail to meet with the financial requirement of higher education. Third World countries badly need to change education systems and structures with the following things in mind:

- Production of highly skill-oriented technical engineers rather than academic engineers.
- Introduction of self-revenue generation scheme in institutes and universities for investment in Research and Development.
- Developing measures to attract bright students into faculty and stop braindrain.
- Integrated approach in education system.
- Removing prejudice and performance in education management and budget allocation to the institutes.

Proper use of products of higher education, in planning and execution – in this regard it shall be very right proposition to refer Dr S. Basu's observation made in his article that even in project specific matters in government, authority rests with bureaucracy causing thereby returns of higher education to marginal level. We can cite different recommendations of different high power committees:

(1) Administrative Reforms Committee (ARC) of Moraraji Desai and K. Hanumanthaiya recommended that "All posts in a factional area whether in field or at headquarters or in the secretariat should be staffed by members of the corresponding functional services...",

(2) ARC of West Bengal headed by Dr. Ashoke Mitra, M.P. recommended that "the technical head, whether already holding the position of ex-officio secretary or otherwise, should be formally designated as the secretary to the department...". Of course, this practice may be coupled with open administration structure in order to derive maximum benefits.

At a symposium on HRD policy conducted by the international Institute of Management Science, Calcutta at New Delhi – YMCA, Dr. A. Dasgupta, emeritus Professor of the University of Delhi confessed that all-round development of his department was not possible as his departmental advisory-cum-governing body was full of non-departmental professors. Such type of exploitation originated administration is existing in our government and is mainly responsible for the fact that though "we have progressed in the field of science and technology, but that has not changed the condition of the people in general" (an anguish of our ex-Prime Minister Indira Gandhi). We are in highly need of better human resources in technical departments. In this scenario, it is believed the hope rests with ICI.

Table 3.3: R&D Expenditure

Country	R&D expenditure (% of GNP)	Scientists & engineers per million population
USA	2.6	3,317
Japan	2.8	5,829
Europe	2.0	1,665
USSR	6.2	5,387
Developing Nations	0.4	158

(a) Based on 1990 data

Country	Public expenditure per pupil in US$
Developed Nations	1983
Sub-Saharan Africa	70
Eastern Asia	55

3.3 ICI VERSUS CONVENTIONAL UNIVERSITIES

Cost-wise

In order to find how best and cost-effective is the ICI over conventional institutes at the primary level, we can make a comparison between NERIST and conventional institutes. We assume expenditure incurred per student as the parameter for such comparison. The expenditure figures of NERIST are portrayed in Fig. (3.6) for a period over 1992-1996. NERIST is typically a 3-in-1 institute, in which ITI, Polytechnic and Graduate and Postgraduate levels of studies are integrated. The data of NERIST is extended to conventional institutes in the following means:

1. Non-Recurring would be Expenditure in 3 Conventional (ITI + Polytechnic + Graduate and Postgraduate) institutes = Building Cost of NERIST + Equipment Cost × P (1)

   Wherein it is assumed that (i) building cost remains constant being proportional to students, staff and faculty strength and (ii) equipment cost in conventional institute p (p>1) times of NERIST

2. Recurring would be expenditure of three conventional institutes, that is (Salary–other costs of NERIST) × P (2)

From computations based on equations (1) and (2) one finds the would-be expenditure as indicated in the bar chart of Figs. (3.6 & 3.7). Fig. (3.7) compares the expenditure of NERIST with that of conventional institutes.

As suggested by Natarajan (1994), financial indicators RP/TP (Revenue or Recurring Payments/Total Payments), NRP/TP (Non-recurring Payments/Total Payments), BP/NRP (Building Payments/Non-recurring Payments) and EP/NRP (Equipment Payments/Non-recurring Payments) are depicted in Fig. (3.8) to compare two conventional institutes, namely, HU (Hyderabad University) and PU (Pondicherry University) with non-conventional institute, NERIST. We find that as per financial expenditure, NERIST is comparable to other conventional institute. Equipment expenditure of NERIST is more than HU and PU; whereas building expenditure is less than HU.

SWOT Analysis

SWOT Analysis of Modular Technical Education

Modular technical education is a multi-entry multi-output (MEMO) system. The modular technical education scheme is illustrated in Fig. (3.9).

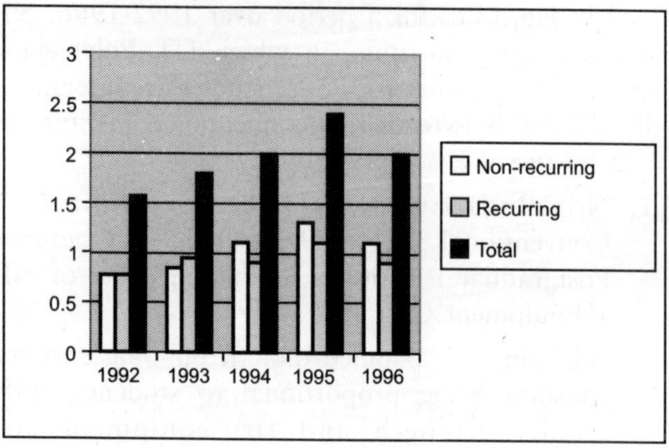

Fig. 3.6: Expenditure per student in NERIST in Rs lacs in NERIST

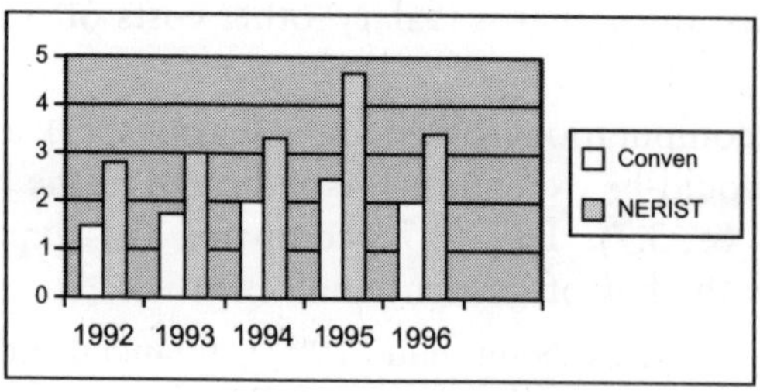

	Conventional	NERIST
1992	1.5	2.8
1993	1.75	3
1994	2	3.3
1995	2.5	4.7
1996	2	3.4

Fig. 3.7: Expenditure per students in Rs lacs

In the scheme class 10 passed students are admitted to two years' Base Module or Certificate Module. Based on merit and/ or percentage of seats reserved for upward mobility, some students move to the next module known as Diploma Module, which is again of two years duration. 10+2 passed students and ITI students are allowed to take lateral entry in Diploma Module to fill the seats vacated by terminal students of Base

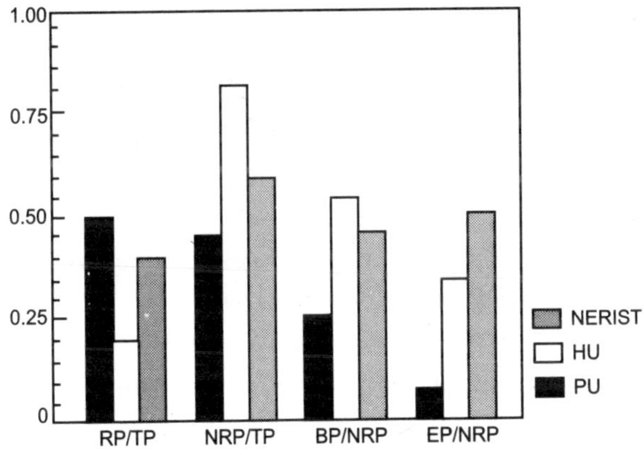

Fig. 3.8: Expenditure Comparison Year-1990-91

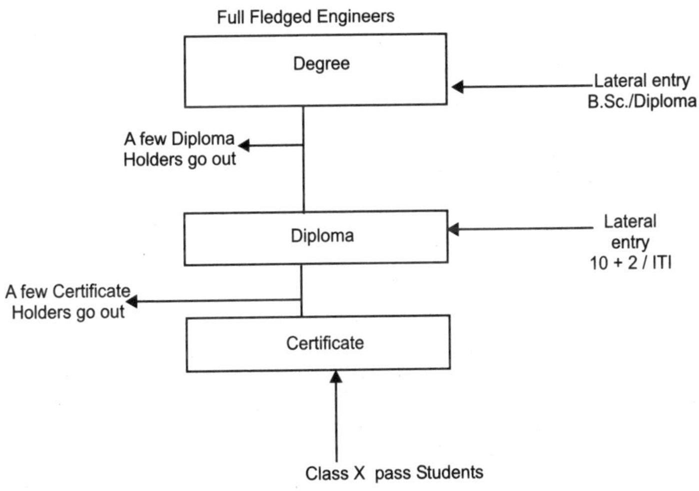

Fig. 3.9: Modular System

Module. At the end of diploma, again a few students have to go out with diploma and remaining students get vertical admission in the next module known as Degree Module which is again of two years duration. Lateral entry is taken into degree module from students of B.Sc. and diploma.

The Lateral entry students both at the diploma and the degree modules are given some bridge courses to bring them at par with vertical entry students.

The modular technical education has the following SWOT parameters:

Strength

- A single Institute produces engineers at different levels from Certificate to Degree.
- The system is a cost-effective higher education system.
- The optimal utilization of man-machine-material-money resources is possible in the system.
- Modular scheme is an integrated approach to higher education.
- Continuous exposure of students since their early age in experiments makes them more experiment oriented.

Weakness

- When same faculty members teach at different modules, the teaching at some levels may not be appropriate.
- Syllabus for modular education is yet to be standardized at the national level. Due to MEMO scheme, overlapping of courses are unavoidable causing some courses being over taught and some courses lesser taught.

Opportunities

- Due to the availability of students at different technical levels, Institute-Cum-Industry (ICI) scheme could be implemented easily. This will make institutes financially self-sustained and self-supporting.
- Conversion of technical education into ICI may attract bright students to join teaching profession by virtue of ICI's ability to pay higher perks and to provide better infrastructure and opportunities for professional growth.

Threats

- The modular concept lies on MEMO operation. Students often take admission in the Base.
- Module thinking that they shall go out as degree engineers. The pressure on this from students union may cause terminality at the end of Base and Diploma Module to hamper, thereby destroying the system itself.
- There remains a high probability of an unworthy nexus between students and teachers, for vertical mobility.
- If man-machine-materials are not optimally used and integrated, overspending in conventional institutes may occur.

The SWOT analysis suggests that modular technical education needs wider acceptance and support and experiment for making it a viable alternative to conventional higher education. However, design of a course structure and syllabus for modular technical education is a big challenge. But it can be overcome.

SWOT Analysis of Private Technical Institutes

Strength

- Higher education is not at the cost of state funding.
- Initiatives are outside the purview of government bureaucratic rules and procedures.
- Education is at corporate like environment rather than at conventional educational environment.

Weakness

- Laboratories and physical infrastructures may not be at par with those of government, government aided institutes.
- Profit the only motive may cause immature death of private institutes.
- Profit motives may enforce the private institutes to admit weak but rich students at the cost of meritorious but poor students.

Opportunities

- Society gets more and more technical manpower.
- Private initiatives may both be better profit making industries and institutes for human resource generation—this shall be ICI revolution.
- Competitiveness in education may enhance the productivity and the quality of education.
- More technical manpower may lead to growth of entrepreneurs in society.

Threats

- Profit motives may lead to recruit less and sub-standard and incompetent faculty members causing quality of education to fall down.
- More technical manpower may cause more unemployment which may lead to the death of private institutes.
- In private colleges, priorities of authorities if any are directed towards the development of secured financial and business system only, that may cause the quality of education to degrade.

Notes

1. *NERIST Project Report* of Working Group Headed by Prof. A. Bhattacharjee, JU, Calcutta.
2. C.T. Bhunia, Letters to the Editor, *The Stateman Patrika*, Sept. '92.
3. C.T. Bhunia's Lecture on ICI at *NTTF Seminar*, 1993.
4. M. Abdus Salam, "Science, Technology and Science Education in the Development of the South", 1991, *The Third World Academy of Science,* p. 60.
5. Report; *The New Internationalist*, U.K., 1993, pp. 18-19.
6. Nancy DiTemase et al., "Degrees and Diversity at Work", *IEEE Spectrum USA*, 1994, pp. 38-40.
7. C.T. Bhunia, "Institute-cum-Industry", *University News*, Aug. 1994, pp. 11-14.
8. C.T. Bhunia et al., A model structure of ICI ... Engg; Prac ISTE National Seminar-cum-Workshop on Management of Technical Education, Bhopal 1995, pp. 1-7.

9. C.T. Bhunia et al., "ICI Revisited", *University News*, Nov. 1995, pp. 1-4, 10.
10. S. Basu, "Education for the 21st Century", *University News*, Nov. 1995, pp. 5-6.
11. C.T. Bhunia, "Institute-cum-Industry", *University News*, Aug. 1994, pp. 11-14.
12. Bill Ratterec, "The Prospects for Teachers", *UNESCO Courier*, April 1996, p. 26.

References

C.T. Bhunia et al., "ICI Revisited", *University News*, Nov. 1995, pp. 1-4.

C.T. Bhunia et al., A Model Structure of ICI of Electronics and Computer Engineering, Proc ISTE National Seminar Cum Workshop on Management of Technical Education, Bhopal, 1995, pp. 1-7.

C.T. Bhunia, "Institute cum Industry", *University News*, Aug. 1994, pp. 11-14.

C.T. Bhunia, "Person Power Development–Why and How", *CSI Communication*, Feb. 1997.

Constantine N. Anaguostopoulos et al., "Special Report: US Education", *IEEE Spectrum*, April 1998, pp. 26-28.

M.A. Salam, "Science, Technology and Science Education in the Development of South", *The Third World Academy of Science*, May 1991.

R. Narasimhan, "Recounting the Myths and Reality", *The Computers Today*, March 1992.

S. Basu, "Education for 21st Century", *University News*, Nov. 1995, pp. 5-6.

Stener and Freeman, *Management*, 5 Edition, Prentice Hall, pp. 16-17.

Y. Deva Editor's Musings, *IETE Newsletter*, March '98, p. 10.

4 Restructuring Courses (FARE and SARE) for the Quantum Jump and Higher Productivity

4.1. HIGHER EDUCATION: RESTRUCTURING AND PRODUCTIVITY

The world is on the transition from the industry-based and regional or national based society of 19th – 20th century to knowledge-based and "one world one village" or global society in 21st century. This is the advent of the information technology that is due to the convergence of the computer, communication and electronics technologies. In the 21st century, knowledge will be the key, and the fundamental sources of wealth will be knowledge and information rather than raw materials and labour. The *UNESCO Courier* December 1998 issue noted: "A two-kilo cake contains twice as much flour, eggs and sugar as a one-kilo cake. A cake can only be eaten if it's within reach of hungry hands and mouths, and once it's been eaten it's all gone. A copy of a computer program, on the other hand, only has a marginal cost, that of its physical support or its transfer. Internet users thousands of kilometers away from each other can 'consume' it simultaneously. And it doesn't wear out when it has been used. This comparison encapsulates the difference between the industrial economy and the 'knowledge economy', which is also known variously as the 'intangible economy', 'the weightless economy', the 'immaterial economy' or simply the 'new economy'. In this economy, ideas, images and knowledge are more prominent than physical products, machines and raw materials. Just as harnessing energy spawned industrial society, so mastery of data processing and transmission has given rise to the knowledge economy. It is particularly strong in four leading sectors: information and communication technologies, intellectual property—patents, brand-names, advertising and financial services; databases and recreational services; biotechnology." It is often said if we can transport lots of bits so easily and so quickly and so economically, there is no need to transport raw materials and physical labor. Kevin Kelly wrote in his article "New Rules for the New Economy" published in the *Wired* magazine of USA that "The Law of Displacement: materials are displaced by information, mass by bits, the old economic dynamics by network behavior." Measuring of the economic value of knowledge is still a complex job and a big challenge. But some works have been done. In 1962 Fritz Machlup (Gerardo et al., 1999) of USA, based on 1958 data, concluded that 34.5% of the Gross National Product in the United States could be allocated to the information sector. Some others reports of USA say: (a) in 1977 information sector was 25.1% of the Gross Domestic Product and generated 43% of all corporate profits, and (b) in 1992 information technology and communications sectors had grown to 10 % of the Gross National Product. A work reported that information might be treated as a fundamental unit of nature. Tomorrow the industry will be knowledge industry where knowledge workers may be quite expensive but the most expandable of all. A report (Constantine N. Anagnostopoulos et al., 1998) says: "Education seems more closely tied than ever to an individual's economic success, according to a 1996 study by Frank Levy, Professor of urban economics at the Massachusetts Institute of Technology (MIT), in Cambridge." Commenting over the knowledge society Peter Drucker wrote (Yashwant Deva, 1998): "The leading social groups of the knowledge society will be knowledge workers and knowledge executives who know how to allocate knowledge to productive use, just as the capitalists knew how to allocate capital to productive use .... Yet, unlike the employees under Capitalism, they will own both, the means of production and the tools of production." Daniel Bell proposed, "the crucial point about a post-industrial society is that knowledge and information become the strategic and transforming resources of the society, just as capital and labor have been the strategic and transforming resources of the industrial society." This being the position, the slogan or the mantra (Gerardo et al., 1999) for competitive advantages shall be: (1) "Innovate, Seize the opportunity and Change the rules", and (2) "Learn faster than your competitors." **Innovation** and **Rapid Learning** are the pillars of 21st century. This needs a national "transformation process that is revolutionary in result, but evolutionary in execution."

The mantra of getting competitive edge in the age of liberalization and globalization is "Lead or Follow." Those who want to be follower, they shall continue to remain so years after years. This is because of the simple law of competition that a follower or a borrower country can never get front running technology from the country of export, what they at best can expect is nothing but near obsolete technology and systems. Therefore, going for "lead" is the best mantra of the present days' competitive advantages. Poor countries like India, has thus to go for a "lead" through improved human resources generation in a process of evolution which shall be innovative and rapid. Till today human generation is not done at factory but at the institutions of higher learning and research like Universities, Engineering and Medical colleges/institutes etc. The speculation of "self-designing beings" that would continue to improve themselves "at an ever increasing rate" (Stephen Hawkins, 1995) by the process of machinization of animals is still a mere theory. Under such situations, the reduced budget allocation for the higher education, implemented in recent past in many poor countries, is not beyond the purview of questions and criticisms.

The Case of India

Since 1992 India had taken part in the liberalization, privatization and globalization process. So India needed to improve human resources particularly in technical/higher education and research. But in international standing of higher education and research, not only India's position is poor but also it is becoming poorer day by day. Irony is that this picture has emerged after India's taking part in liberalization process, whereas would be picture should have been the other way around. There are different parameters to see the position of Human Resources, like Human Resources Index (HRI) defined by the United Nations Organization (UNO), etc. HRI of course takes care of elementary education and higher education among other things. In terms of HDI (Human Development Index) of 1998 and 1999 India's positions were respectively 138th and 132nd out of 174 nations (*The Telegraph*, 1999). For the purpose of higher education and research, we may analyze based on other more appropriate parameters. One such parameter is the number of research publications in the international referred journals. Table (4.1) lists data (Tibor et al., 1999) of share of publications in the world's total. It is seen that India's position has shifted from 10th position during 1984-1989 to 12th position during 1990-1995 with a –12.61 growth rate over the period. The situation has been further complicated by the budget cut on higher education. The effect is negative one with a chain reaction (Fig. 4.1).

Table 4.1: Share of Total World Publication

Country	% share in 1984-89	% share in 1990-95	Growth
USA	36.52	35.82	-1.92
UK	9.21	9.24	0.325
Japan	7.37	8.67	17.64
Germany	6.22	7.42	19.3
France	5.17	5.88	14
USSR /Russia	6.85	4.97	-27.45
Canada	4.66	4.77	2.36
Italy	2.69	3.49	29.74
Australia	2.27	2.40	5.73
Netherlands	2.01	2.40	19.40
Spain	1.21	2.08	71.9
India	2.22	1.94	-12.61

It is ample clear that India is not following the correct path to become a leader in the world of globalization. In poor countries and therefore in India also, it is often assumed that higher education is costly. Thus state funding of higher education is not appropriate at the cost of other social

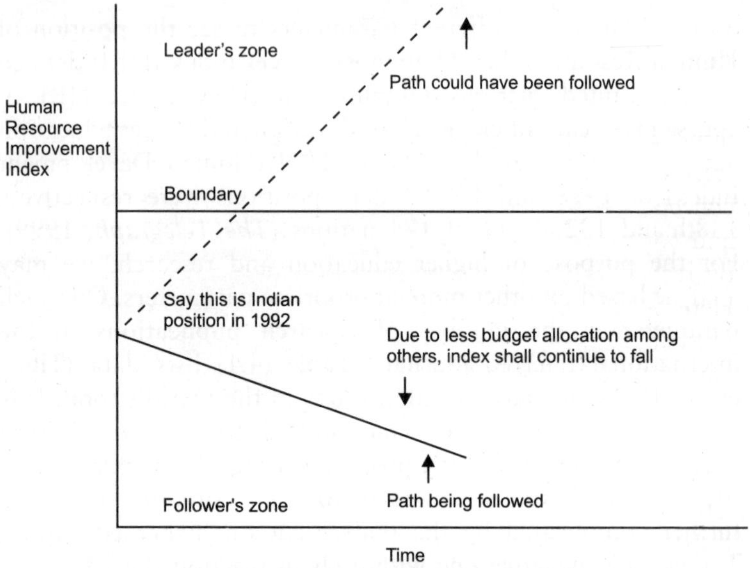

Fig. 4.1: Effect of budget cut or higher education

infrastructure like basic education, health, etc. As per Noble Prize Winner Professor Amartya Sen, any attempt to cut budget for social infrastructure shall be counter-productive, we must not go for that. But we must analyze whether higher education is really costly in India, and if so, what are the reasons for that and must find path to remain out of these reasons. Higher education in India is costly because of the several reasons:

1. Indian, and for that purposes most or all of the poor countries' education system and structure are copied or borrowed from advanced countries. We have no innovative system and structure of our own to meet with our environment and requirements (Bhunia, 1994, 1995, 1996, 1999).
2. Investment return on higher education in poor countries including India is low.

3. Imbalance and improper fund allocation to the institutes.

FARE and SARE

Undoubtedly, we need to have innovative and friendly (in terms of economy, acceptability, operation and affordability, etc.) education systems and structures. In this regard the concept of Institute-Cum-Industry (ICI) is well documented and surveyed (Bhunia). ICI is an innovative proposal mainly on restructure of institutes and integrated technical education. Here we propose some innovative education pattern. In the present-day pattern of education, all the students admitted in any course have to undergo study for a fixed period of time, irrespective of student's ability. Even if a student can amply able to learn all about the course in the shorter period, he is not supposed to do so. Similarly, a less meritorious student is hard pressed by the system itself to complete the course on the fixed time. To overcome the problem and to make our technical education appropriate to the globalization process that needs fast learning, we suggest that for the courses of B.Tech./B.E., we can have two groups:

1. FARE (Fast And Rapid Education) where Fast refers to time duration and Rapid refers to impact of education. FARE for B.Tech./B.E. after 10+2 may be of minimum 3 and maximum 3.5 years duration and shall be allotted to a group of capable students based on merit and choice.
2. SARE (Slow And Recurring Education) where Slow and Recurring respectively refers to time duration and impact of education. SARE for B.Tech./B.E. after 10+2 may be of minimum 5 years and maximum 6 years duration and shall be allotted to the less meritorious students.

FARE is for "learn fast" jargon. Nowadays the students of NRI category and others on capitation fees are being admitted in the technical education, hardly considering the merit. SARE is therefore may be an actual requirement.

Investment Return of Higher Education

It is often said that the investment return of higher education is less or marginal. Work of Shanmugam and Madheswaran (1998) reported, "The marginal rates for the college and university studies in India are lower than the returns for below college level studies. Therefore, more investments and higher subsidies on the education below college level would be more beneficial for both individual and society than that on higher education." But in this study, only individual income was considered for the calculation of return. But with higher education more emphasis would be given to the national income than the individual income. For example, an engineer's monthly salary is not the only return, but his service in terms of production in the factory, development of techniques and systems (that may be assumed as income of nation through his service) are the major returns. A less salaried engineer often contributes to these major returns rather high salaried engineer. Besides, the same work of Shanmugam and Madheswaram reported, "Higher earnings are associated with the higher levels of education." This observation does go against their conclusion on investment return noted above.

The main reason for low investment return to higher education is actually due to the two things: (a) brain drain and (b) non-involvement of professional persons in the policy framing of even project specific matters.

The gravity of the problem caused by the brain drain shall minimize if the people migrating abroad shall even marginally investment in nation building. Nowadays, NRIs (Non-Resident Indians) are participating in the national projects and developments. This is encouraging. At the same time, we have to do something at least to reduce brain drain if not stop it fully. It will be pertaining to mention here a report of the *IEEE Spectrum* (Nancy, 1994) that higher degree holders are more innovative in nature. Higher perks and pay and freedom in work place of professional persons are the major issues needed to be considered seriously to reduce brain drain.

Non-utilization of professional persons in policy making is serious in nature in poor countries. Due to this, professional innovation and inventions are on decline trend in these countries, causing investment return more hard to higher education. We quote here Said (1999) about academic freedom, "Only there could collective learning and the development of knowledge occur and, as in recent years we have discovered, it could occur only if academic freedom from non-academic authority was somehow guaranteed and could prevail."

Measuring Productivity of the Institutes

In order to judge the quality and the capability of the institutes we often do mistakes by seeing the products rather than productivity. Some institutes claim superiority on the basis of the export quality production of engineers. But at what input they do so? Productivity, which is the output, divided by the input, is the appropriate parameter for assessment of the institutes. We define below two productivity factors for assessment:

(a) Productivity for human resources production

= [{(Average number of passed out students – Average number of unemployed students of the lot – Average number of brain drain of the lot) ÷ Average yearly income per students} + {Average number brain drain ÷ Average yearly donation or investment made by a brain drain}]/Average yearly spending for the education.

(b) Productivity for research production

= {Average number of yearly publications in referred journals/Conferences + Average number of yearly patents}/Average yearly spending on research.

The above-defined two parameters may be used for distribution of budget and funds to the institutes.

Conclusion

Any move to limit higher education and research by any means shall be counter-productive for growth and prosperity of any nation. The argument that poor countries should not and cannot bear the high cost of higher education, and that too at the expenses of elementary education and basic health, etc., is sound to hear at the first glance. The proper analysis of this argument and whether the higher education is really costly and if so what are the reasons behind that need to be examined before taking a decision. In the paper we have done a critical review of these things, and came to the conclusion that poor countries should restructure the higher education in the form of ICI, FARE and SARE and take some policy decision to the use of products of higher education in national planning and to reduce brain drain. We have also proposed a means of distribution of funds to the institutes of higher learning and research by a parameter of productivity of the institutes rather than products and names, etc. We believe suggestions made in this paper are in conformity with the tenet of "think global, act local" which is often taken as the way of going with liberalization. Reducing higher education in poor countries shall be a first step of suicidal in the age of open economy and information revolution.

4.2 RESTRUCTURING PRIVATE INVESTMENT IN TECHNICAL EDUCATION

After adoption of open economy and the participation in GATT agreement, the higher education in India has taken a new shape. This is mainly due to overwhelming participation and initiatives from the private sectors. But the government policies and regulations apparently lack directions to achieve the benefits out of the would-be and vision-based regulated private participation. The natural consequence has resulted in the imbalances in different forms in the higher education. Before we look into the important imbalances, a general look into the issues arising out of introduction of GATT agreement, a natural attribute of the privatization is desirable.

Review of General Aspects of Technical Education in GATT Scenario

India ranked 141 out of 173 countries in the overall education index in the year 2000. India ranks below even most developing countries in terms of enrolment per 100,000 inhabitants[1-3]. Out of several other parameters behind such a poor position, one was the non-availability of higher education institutes. With private participation, the opportunities of higher studies increases, and this may increase the enrolment figure comparable to other developing countries. Several educational commissions including Kothari Commission argued for active industry and institute interaction for effective research and development. The private institutes sponsored by the industry houses can more efficiently and meaningfully realize the industry institute interaction for fruitful achievements. At the same time, the resource crunch for R & D activities may be overcome by the industry sponsored institutes. Although debatable, it is often said that private sectors are more disciplined and efficient than the Government sectors. This being a case, it is expected that the education will be more efficiently and in more disciplined way be imparted in the private institutes. It is undoubtedly clear that a corporate culture will prevail in the private institutes that are absent in public institutes.

Due to financial crunch, the students of the developing countries could not study at the universities of the developed countries. But due to GATT, the universities of the developed countries are opening branches at the developing countries that will provide a scope to the students of the developing countries to study at the universities of the developed countries at a relatively low cost. Adam Smith said, "It is not from the benevolence of the butcher ... or the baker that we expect our dinner, but from the regard to their own interest." Here lie all theories of investment by private sectors. Profit or in gentle word return on investment as often told in the education sectors, is the ultimate motive. The profit motive has natural attraction for quality degradation. Low teacher-student ratio of the existing private institutes in general has this reflection. However, profit only motive is dangerous and counter-productive in education sectors. As a consequence of ever-increasing marketization of higher education due to GATT, the basic disciplines like physics, chemistry, mathematics, languages, philosophy, history and geography, etc. are not offered in the private institutes and universities. The private investment still is oriented to courses of market demand. This will create an imbalance in the higher education system. In India most of the private engineering colleges offer courses in Computer, Electronics and IT and hardly mother engineering like mechanical, electrical, civil, etc. The imbalance so created will have adverse effect in future both in terms of availability of engineers at proportional level and in related expertise and development. The high tuition fees of higher education in private sectors will encourage only affordable societies to opt for. The meritorious poor students will not benefit from higher education opportunities offered by the private institutes. Is not GATT creating a further gap between haves and have-nots in higher education? Generating scope for higher education for affordable students at the costs of non-affordable but meritorious students is bound to cast poor figure on quality on outputs and cause poor productivity.

Main Issues

The main issues revolve around two things: (a) how to make government to establish institutes of technical higher education as state sectors and (b) how to remove the major imbalances arisen out of the participation of private initiatives. In the present work a few possible solutions are suggested.

The solution of problem (a) lies in proposed Institute-cum-Industries (ICI)[4-12]. The development of human resources development using IT will be another cost-effective measure for the developing nations both in higher technical education as well as primary and elementary level education. We emphasize, as told in Section 1, that critical mass in elementary/primary education must be achieved to go for increasing enrolment in higher technical education. But any attempt to use IT for enhancement in education by just copying the process of other countries particularly developed countries will be an exercise in complete futility. We suggest the would-be approach in our work in the following section.

4.3 RELEVANCY OF USING IT

Privatization, liberalization and globalization are replacing liberty, equality and fraternity all over the world. It does not mean that liberty, equality and fraternity have no relevance in today's society. They are ever alive and their universal appeal shall ever remain for the noble human cause, but privatization, liberalization and globalization shall be other social partners with them in the next century. This is a wave brought forward by a single most technology known as Information Technology (IT). In the last two decades, the world has been gradually shifting from one "I" to another "I", namely, Industrial based society to information based society. As a result, besides economic indicator, GNP and human development index, (HDI) the United Nation Organization (UNO) has assumed one more indicator known as "Information rich" and "Information poor" to classify countries in the world. Due to information exploration, today knowledge has become power, and hence saleable. As per Deva, knowledge and information are defined as:

Raw Data when processed = Information

Information – Noise (example: unwanted information/ information oversupply, misinformation) = Intelligence

Intelligence + Experience = Knowledge

Knowledge + Judgement = Wisdom

Although, it is foreseen that knowledge based machines may play a significant role in industries in coming days, yet it is HUMAN who shall remain the driver. One major attribute of human resource is knowledge which is a derivative of information. This is the reason why since the last decade the Human Resource Development (HRD) has become the focal point in management. Human Resource is the key of success. Peter Drucker once said, "The proper or improper use of different factors of production depends UPON THE WISHES OF HUMAN RESOURCES. Hence, besides other resources, human resources need more development." Application of IT brings attitudinal, qualitative and quantitative changes in performance of human resources. The impact of information technology is spearheaded over all areas of management: production, planning, administration, marketing, co-ordination, research and development, human resources development, etc. Telemarketing, Telebanking, Teleresearching, Telemailing,

Teleconferencing. Teleadvertisement, Teletraining and Telecommuting, are to name a few applications of IT in management and business. The benefit of use of IT are immense. Bell emphasized the benefits on STS (space, time and scale). Productivity and growth become independent of the location of raw materials. With information infrastructure, other factors shall now determine the location of activities. IT has reduced "NO TIME" problem. Efficient use of time is possible with application of IT in hand, "swift movement of capital and slow movement of people" have added flexibility, efficiency and effectiveness in business towards globalization process. Richard S. Sloma in his book *No Nonsense Management* observed that "Your true adversary is time." The impact of IT application on time or mobility of managers can be defined by an equation:

Volume of information available on managers' desk ×
Volume of mobility of managers = Constant.

The stated equation means more is the information available on the desk, less is the required mobility of management. IT provides competitive advantages in business and economy. Today, not only better, but faster has become another parameter of success. In a real sense, the advantage is titled towards those who are using IT in their work, activities and business. Application of IT in business and management, and benefits achieved out of this have very much a chicken and egg affair. IT use and production both typically require supporting infrastructure like telecommunication networks, human resources, research and development capabilities.

IT application brings advantages of learning in leisure time and as lifetime experiences. Satellites (LEO, MEO, GEO), VSAT, Cable TV, Radio and TV are other means of such experiences of learning. Due to the use of IT, there has been paradigm shifts in training and education process. New shifts are training and courses on demand, lifelong and year round learning, global education everywhere and at any time, and students as a customer rather than product, and library referencing through Internet and other networks. Application of audio-visuals displays in training is facilitating both trainers and trainees to improve by a common finding that people recall 20% of what they hear, 30% of what they see and 50% of what they see and hear. Any organization intending to compete through knowledge or to become a knowledge industry, should develop IT oriented training, education and development programme.

Information Technology is exerting growing impacts on HRD process by three major ways: effectiveness (enhancing capability of doing right things), efficiency (improving capability of doing things right) and excellence (improving satisfaction, decision making and creativeness). It is often argued that managers, bureaucrats and leaders are respectively effective, efficient and excellent. IT has therefore impact on human resources at all level of functionaries. The important tools of IT which are bringing impacts on these improvements are expert system, MIS (Management Information System) and DSS (Decision Support System).

Any organization intending to compete through knowledge or to become a knowledge industry, should develop IT oriented training, education and development programme.

Expert System

The field of Artificial Intelligence (AI) actually made the soil for Expert System (ES). Out of many exotic and awe-inspiring applications of AI, the expert system is one. The ES while becomes the "great white hope" of Information Technology (IT) to many, yet to some others it appears as a modified version of the "yellow peril." However, the ES is a computer system, basically a software which like a human expert, should know more and more about less and less. It will be able to correctly inference the knowledge base within the system with required inputs to suggest a solution to a problem. The success of any ES is based on the extent and the equality of the "Knowledge base", and the "human window." The success of ES can also be measured by how genuinely the system is "user-friendly."

However, the British computer society defines ES as "the embodiment within a computer of knowledge based component, from an expert skill, in such a form that the system can offer intelligent advice or take an intelligent decision about a processing function. A desirable additional characteristic, which would consider fundamental, is the capability of the system, on demand, to justify its own line of reasoning in a manner directly intelligible to the inquirer. The style adopted to attain these characteristics is rule-based programming."

Where should the expert system be used? Is it applicable to all problems? This is a serious question. There are many options in this regard. But the main thing is that whether the ES is required to solve a problem, depends on the type of the problem itself. As per Prof. Richard Forsy (Table. 1) lists the areas of applicability versus non-applicability of the ES. However, a few important areas of application by name are: (1) chemical analysis, (2) medical diagnosis, (3) horoscope making, (4) intelligent front ends processor (where an ES is developed to act as an expert on the working an another computer package, (5) computer based tutorial system/intelligent tutorial system (ITS) (thereby drastically changing the education system from school based to home based), and (6) the "infinite desk" for managers (fully office automation), etc.

Although the main two units of any ES are the knowledge-based and the inference engine, yet another two units are required to support a complete architecture of any ES which are knowledge acquisition unit and the explanatory interface unit.

The inference engine is the thinking machine and the knowledge base is that about which the engine is to think. The knowledge base is made of short-term information (i.e. facts or assertions which may change rapidly) and long-term information (i.e. rules which state how to formulate new facts or hypotheses from the present knowledge). The knowledge base differs from conventional database methodology in the sense that the knowledge base is more creative. Unlike data base, it always tries to fill in the missing information.

The explanatory unit is the user interface so that the user at any time can enquire about any step and process, etc. to the ES.

The most important tool to design an ES is the programming language. The programming languages may be classified broadly in two groups as the symbolic language (PROLOG LISP) and the algorithmic language (BASIC, C, FORTRAN, etc). There is widespread feeling that all expert systems have to be written either in LISP or in PROLOG. However, this is not true. Expert system can also be well developed in using C, FORTRAN 77, etc.

The future of the knowledge industry rests on: (i) shifting the world from the energy machine (industrial revolution) to information machine (intelligent computer, the machine brain), (ii) coupling the energy devices (i.e. robots are coming), (iii) the emergence of IT through the marriage of computer and communication, which is often known as communication, (iv) developing expert systems, and (v) expanding intellectual technologies.

Decision-making process is involved at each and every level of management process. Decision-making process requires informative data and managers' skill and vision to make it both effective and efficient.

It is seen that the expert system has a promising role in industrialization of knowledge. As such expert system may help us to some extent. But creating human serving expert system has a negative consequence on the human psyche, and the human dignity, and there are chances of a new set of complexities of the problems that are still less understood.

Whatever may be the situation, no machine expert can make human expert obsolete as the human brain is ever fertile and a mystery.

Management Information System

Decision-making process is involved at each and every level of management process. Decision-making process requires informative data and managers skill and vision to make it both effective and efficient. With the use of IT, nowadays, management is poised to use MIS (Management Information System) as a tool for management decision-making process. Earlier days, management also used to use information systems supplied by many assistants. Assistants used to do manual preparation of data for managerial use in files and papers. The human prepared information system has become obsolete with evolution of MIS. MIS has a number of advantages over man made paper-based earlier systems for managerial applications. Table (4.2) gives a comparison of these two forms of information systems. In some literature earlier form of management information system is called as information system, whereas computerized MIS is called as formal MIS.

What is MIS? Different experts define MIS in may different forms. One such definition is, "a formal method of making available to management the accurate and timely information necessary to facilitate the decision making process and enable the organization's planning, control and operational functions to be carried out effectively." However, we can find a simple definition of MIS based on the goals of MIS. The objective of MIS is to support managerial decision making process to make it effective and efficient one. Thus MIS aids management by taking and applying full proof decision at the right time to the right proposition. MIS may be defined as a powerful support system available to managers to facilitate decision making process. MIS should have the following characteristics:

- It should provide sufficient information to the managers. Less information may lead to an inappropriate decision being taken.
- It should provide relevant information. Unwanted information may lead to take frustrated decision. Unwanted information is a kind of noise. Characteristics mentioned above may be termed as necessary and sufficient condition of a standardized MIS.

- It should provide flexibility. This means that managers should be able to access information as per their desired or required fashion.
- It should provide accurate information. Inaccurate information may lead to take a wrong decision. More accurate the information is, more accurate will be the decision taken on its basis.
- It should provide timely information. Out of time and delay are negative aspects of today's management.
- It should be available to managers without any constraints of space and time (i.e. availability at any time). It should support manager mobility.
- It should be secured enough against intentional modifications and/or deliberate destruction by opponents and/or ompetitors.

MIS is applicable to only organizations which are having appropriate computer and communication systems, access to appropriate computer/data networks, less but quite skillfull computer assistants/operators and managers with appropriate skill to use, operate, understand and interact with MIS. While the first two requirements require "improved machine systems" and/or "accessing facilities to computer networks", the latter two requirements require "improved human resources" in the organization. Both the improvements are essentials for use of MIS. Fulfillment of improved human resources and improvement machines are essential. Total managerial skill or human resource skill is often defined as technical skill (technological subsystem of HRD), conceptual skill (knowledge, experience and information) and behavior skill (man to man relation).

> MIS is "a formal method of making available to management the accurate and timely information necessary to facilitate the decision-making process and enable the organization's planning, control and operational functions to be carried out effectively."

Any design, whether hardware or software, must conform to Qualibility where:

Qualibility = Quality + Reliability

Qualibility = refer to the design as per standard specification Reliability refers to the ability of the system to work within a specified boundary at a given environment within a specified life time. From these definitions it is simply understood that these two are hardly different from each other from conceptual point of view and practical consideration. If a designed system cannot work (i.e. unreliable), then how is it designed as per standard specification? It is the specified standard which lies in between the two. Therefore, qualibility is a more appropriate aspect of any design. It has two parameters:

(1) Standard specification which may be constant (i.e. aspects of quality).

(2) Variable specification (i.e. aspect or reliability).

Therefore, we need today to have qualibility MIS for managers. MIS must be designed to conform with requirement of any organization. MIS may have some same constant specification for all organizations, but it must have at the same time some variable specifications which vary from organization to organization. MIS designers must provide this facility.

As per Robert G. Murdick, conventional design step of MIS are:

- An initial survey and defining the problems thereon.
- A conceptual design and defining methodology.
- A principal design.
- A practical design.
- Final design and implementation.

MIS is for upgradation of management decision and managerial skill. It will be more so as the field of AI (Artificial Intelligence) progresses. MIS and Expert systems and AI are the tools of automated management of organization. The limiting target of such automation is "Machination of Animals" and "Animalization of Machines," but perhaps never without direct or indirect involvement of human resources.

IT and Nature

It is often called that nature is the best manager. First law of natural law based management is known as a principal of least action which aims to "accomplish most with least effort." The tools of IT, namely MIS and ES are what people can use to achieve the goal with least effort and loss of energy. Rest and activity and success without strain are the other two laws of natural law based management. With IT, global information can be available to managers' desks and tools like video conferencing (man to man logical interaction) being the rule of the days, managers achieve success without strainful travels and hard work. IT supports natural law based management in full and whole.

Shanon defined information as the "reduction of uncertainty". Information thereby being a "meta resource" of decision-making process, IT based management becomes a management of "reduction of failures."

Recently, Tom Stonier has speculated in his work *Information and Internal Structure of the Universe* that there is an analogy between mass/matter, energy/heat and information/ order of an organization. It has been argued that information (I) resident in any organization is proportional to the order (O) of the organization.

$$I = C.O.$$

where C is the constant of proportionality. If this relation exists, there may be a possibility of interchangeability of information with energy (information based society with industrial based society), and the exchange rate could be:

I Joule per degree Kelvin = 1023 bits of information.

It may raise many criticisms and questions, but there is a direction which if proved correct in future, may lead to a conclusion that information is not something external of nature, but a fundamental unit of nature. In that case, we may enter into a world of nth dimension. In such an era, people shall be unable to resist the temptation to improve human characteristics like increased memory, etc. "Self designing beings" shall be possible with use of IT. "Self designing beings" who would continue to improve themselves "at an ever increasing rate" may be ever fertilized human resources of any organization, but they may bring major social, organizational and political conflicts too. But there is always a natural limit. Let us hope for the best.

> It is often called that nature is the best manager. First law of natural law based management is known as a principal of least action which aims to "accomplish most with least effort."

Information Technology deals with information collection processing and transformation. It is therefore 2C+E = computer + communication + Electronics (consumer). Although IT has profound impact on economy, society, growth and productivity, the developing countries are yet to explore the technology. There is a vast unequal use of IT. Gradually a situation of "Lead" follow or "get out of the way" is coming up. Our exercise with "Cheap Labour" force has failed. Now is the time to "follow or lead" with improved human resource. Prospective look on HRD in India shall have the slogans of working with multinationals, learn from challenges, and use of IT.

4.4 HOW TO APPLY IT/E-LEARNING AS EXAMPLE IN INDIA

How to achieve critical mass as told in Section 1

E-learning as a case study in India

Revolution or evolution, let it remain an academic debate, but the fact is that IT (Information Technology) in practice has changed many faces of the society to its advantages. More than any period in recorded history, today's IT has transformed society to some unprecedented era. Society has been creating technology, but with IT, the technology is creating a rapidly changing new society. The information consumption is becoming order of the society. E-business, e-commerce, e-marketing (tele-marketing), e-shopping (tele-shopping), e-mail, e-journal, e-government, e-learning and so many other e-applications, IT has gifted this world. Change is to the only thing in nature that remains constant. Thus in pace with the change, every individual, every organization and every nation must learn to move and change. Only caution that needs to be taken is that in the name of change, any action if taken without properly analyzing the consequences of the change in the own socio-economic-political environment may become counter-productive. In this regard, it may not be incorrect to refer to the example of the success story and the failure story of the participation in liberalization, privatization and globalization (LPG) processes respectively of South Korea and Brazil. It is essential to welcome time tested new technology and to move with changes, but that must be done in "Our way and Our means to meet Our local systems"(3O system) but surely not just copying from the others and becoming copy masters. Judicious selection, Appropriate methodology, Selective changes and Timely adoption (JAST) should be the basic dimension for moving with the changes. In this scenario, an investigation is desirable for e-learning approaches in India that is understood to be coming in a big way.

SWOT analysis on e-learning

Strength

- With e-learning system, Electronic Universities, Virtual Institutes, Cyberspace Schools may come up as technological replacement of conventional /traditional universities, institutes and schools. Opening non- traditional paths for teaching and learning/ FAST and UNIVERSAL access universities are e-universities.
- Earn a degree in shortest period of time/Fast track education.
- Anywhere, anytime education/provides users immense flexibilities . Unlike fixed university hours, the students can learn at his/her leisure time, off time. Employed persons face no problem of pursuing education with e-learning. With e-learning individualization or personalization of learning is possible.
- Wide geographical coverage for providing education unlike conventional geographically limited universities/ remoteness is overcome in e-universities.

- Education/learning at home/at friend's house/at club/ at Cyber café is possible/move or no move education is at the door of the learners.
- Anytime/alltime virtual teacher's presence for all sorts of expertise. Teacher's unavailability and/or dearth of teachers is a no problem issue in e-learning approach.
- Many times interaction approach/ IF-THEN approach. E-learning offers a scope of many times interactive session to learners. In real human interaction, the teachers may get irritated after a few interactions. The servant machine computer network has no human irritation.

Opportunity

- Low cost virtual university using technology may be better affordable particularly for developing countries .
- Paperless, Chalk duster less education/environmentally clearer system of education.
- Generation of e-learning tools and materials are relatively faster, easier and cheaper than traditional books and copies.
- Education adds quality to democracy. With e-learning, education may reach to the remotest of the remote, the poorest of the poor.
- E-learning may add to the productivity to the farmers and the weaker society. If e-learning is available to the villages, improved agriculture techniques, gardening, fisheries and soil processing may be known to the farmers/teaching in regard to population control and basic health and sanitation may be provided at ease and low cost to the farmers and villagers.
- E-learning is a process to accomplish most with least action. The first law of management of nature is the principle of least action and least time that aims to "accomplish most with least effort" and least time. In nature, everything follows the least path of action.

Apple falls from a tree to ground on straight line, waters falls down in straight line, and light travels on straight path, etc.

Weakness

- Until and unless the access of Internet/Network is made available to remote villages and the poor, the scope of e-learning will remain a dream.
- Until and unless the cost of PC and accessories for e-learning is made affordable to the common mass and the poor, the e-learning scope will be confined to the elite societies only.
- Electricity has yet to reach most of the villages of the developing nations. How will then e-learning be made possible to the villages and the remote people?
- The present mode of e-learning is mostly English. Will it suit the common people? Elementary/Primary and even to large extent secondary education is not possible without making e-learning mode in mother tongue.
- Physical experiment particularly in Science and Technology and Medical is not possible with e-learning. Learn by doing is absent in e-learning.
- Knowledge grows day by day, even exponentially. How then the data base of e-learning will cope with growing knowledge volumes? Of course, very very high or ultra dense memory systems are being developed, improved data compression techniques are being developed, the concept of using data mining in e-learning is being explored, yet weakness in this regard remains an issue to be resolved.
- Repetitive application of e-learning materials is cost effective for developing countries. The UNESCO Courier December 1998 by a beautiful analogy compared the nature of the wealth of the different ages: "A two-kilo cake contains twice as much flour,

eggs and sugar as a one-kilo cake. A cake can only be eaten if it's within reach of hungry hands and mouths, and once it's been eaten it's all gone. A copy of a computer program, on the other hand, only has a marginal cost, that of its physical support or its transfer. Internet users thousands of kilometers away from each other can 'consume' it simultaneously. And it doesn't wear out when it's been used."

Threats

- E-learning is basically machine based and machine oriented. Lack of human touch, emotion, love and affection may not attain desired success. When a problem becomes difficult to a learner and/or when a problem becomes a cause of irritation to a learner, touch of some humors and artistic expression may make the problem easy. Only teachers' innovation can create such art and humors. This lack of the e-learning may make it unacceptable to learners after a certain level.
- Teaching is not only dissemination of knowledge but is an art also. The art of teaching is individual's ability of creation that is ever fertilized. E-learning can never achieve this ever fertilized art of teaching. Learners may horribly miss the teacher's art of teaching.
- The art of teaching help in generating imagination in students' minds. E-learning can not do so. Imagination power of learners may not ignite in e-learning process at a pace as it is done in teacher's teaching. Like the antibiotic gradually decreases the resistive power of body, the e-learning may decrease the imaginative power of learners.
- Guru-Shishya relation will be absent in e-learning. The society often solves many social problems by the healthy relation of Guru-Shishya. That the society may lose with e-learning. In e-learning the students are customers rather than Shishyas.

- Mechanization in e-learning may augment towards inhuman behavior in the society. Bewilderment, chaotic behavior, selfishness may emerge among the young generations.
- The e-learning may create a social division like that in current digital divide issue. Developed may override the developing. Gap between privileged and unprivileged may be wider.
- E-learning may augment the piracy like that is found in software piracy. Security threats consequently exists that may offer a distorted course to learners. For example virus may change Newton's famous p=mf equation to p=m/f or Einstein's $E= MC^2$ equation to $E=M^2C$ making learners confused and chaotic.
- E-learning has no creative power. Can it write "Where the mind is without fear and the head is held high ....Into that heaven of freedom, Oh God, Let my country awake!" Can it even be written sitting before a computer in a closed AC fitted room? I wonder if e-learning may limit the imagination of great person by making them confined in closed door learning. The difference between the learning in conventional classroom with Guru's touch and e-learning is that between physically kissing your kids and kissing your kids' photographs.
- E-learning may make education a commercial business venture. Consumerism and commoditization of education is the next natural step. Will that make education qualitative?
- Business nature of e-learning may tempt to invest more in machines than in human resources generation. Any attempt to lowering investment on human capital may cause huge loss to any nation. Any invention, innovation, technology is due to man but not otherwise. In an organization when the Managing Director was asked what he wanted to make his organization great, pat came the reply "Process." On

the same question, the Vice President answered: "People", the President's answer was "Good People", meaning people those who are resources.

Optimal Scenario

The SWOT analysis of e-learning clearly demonstrates that e-learning must not be taken and thought of a replacement of conventional teacher's centric education, but as a supplement and value addition to the existing Guru-Shishya system of education in utilizing the bests of both in togetherness. In fact they are inherently tied in their own definitions and for their growth (Fig. 4.2). The e-learning will be based on documented knowledge, whereas teachers' essentiality will remain for creating new knowledge, realizing new research and inventive and innovative knowledge, techniques and ideas. E-learning is for already known knowledge, teachers are for new knowledge. Teachers' power is for circulatory generating new knowledge that will add content to e-learning. Thus existence and growth of e-learning is due to creation of knowledge by the teachers of the society. The survival of e-learning for that matter the conceptuated knowledge society is surely at the hands of knowledge creators, and not on the machines, networks and software.

JAST for e-learning

JAST is not same for all countries. JAST is 3O centric. JAST for e-learning approaches in India to a fair estimate will be as follows:

- J: Apply e-learning for three categories: (i) *elementary & primary education to achieve commendable Human Development Index at UNO, and this should be fully funded by the state (ii) very specialized courses like bio-technology, 4G technology to attain at the international level in technology/ we need quantum jump as we are on an average lagging by 4 to 10 years in technology with international reference / we have dearth of specialized skilled knowledge in those areas and (iii) for affordable persons for courses like*

MCA/MA/M. Sc/MBA at some middle level cost. The scheme may be made profitable to meet the funds required for (i) and (ii).

- A: Methodology should to identify the priority of applying J. It should not be on perception based but on reality based. Perception should not overrule reality. Frankly speaking, on the election days announcing and inaugurating e-learning centers by our leaders is surely not, by any definition, any methodology of applying e-learning for national growth. Indian methodology should be evolved around: (i) making availability of electricity and network access if not all over rural areas but at least at one centre at each village, (ii) ensuring community informatics rigorously by the process of *bringing computer/Network access/Teachers to the villagers rather than asking villagers to go for computer learning* and ensuring generation of critical computer knowledgeable persons, (iii) producing the e-learning content logically understandable to users, like pictures, etc. as is used for displaying weather report on TV news, (iv) contractual engagement of local youths (NOT PRIVATE PARTICIPATION BY TENDER BUSINESS – both white and black) by **Ram Krishna Mission** or similar organizations.
- S: I must highlight the failures of bad selection. In the name of computerization, the beginning was made by replacing typewriters with computers. In name of computerization in offices, the beginning was made by providing a computer to each official without looking into the matter whether it is at all essential for the official or whether at all the official is in position to use computers. What has therefore turned into is that the computer has become a status symbol like a good towel on chair. Selection would have been use of computers for recording data related to files, for larger volume of data with training of

selected groups, then gradually replacing typewriters and providing computers to officials one after another on need base process. This lesson we have to take in e-learning process. Selection should start from near remote to remote to remotest area by gradual spreading (Fig. 4.3). Each centre in each district of each state should be chosen to provide equal development to each state.

- T: Today's mantra for competitive advantages is **"fast is first."** So, time is now and just now only. In Indian culture, it is often noticed that to start with anything, committees, commissions, task forces are constituted, the things that rather than helping the growth exploits and kills the growth. I wonder if there were any committee to design Howrah Bridge, the bridge would not have seen the light of the day till today. To me, committees, commissions and task forces are the powers of impotence of originality, vision and mission looking. No committee, commission or task force is needed, we just need to start of the project.

Conclusion

As was pointed out in the previous section, in nature the sustainable thing is "change." Therefore, it will not be wrong to welcome and adopt e-learning. Moreover, e-learning offers more option, more information and simple transactions in information and knowledge sharing (Fig. 4.4). But we need to know that in USA or in developed nations, there can be left choices before the learners to select either traditional universities/institutes/schools or electronic (virtual) universities/institutes/schools. In India we simply cannot do that, and while adopting changes we have to analyze quality versus quantity. The developed country has the choice to accept or reject, we have to have necessity based. That is how we must be very much judiciously selective. E-learning must not be targeted just for quantity, we have to optimize quantity with quality by hybrid of teachers with e-learning.

The solution that has been attempted in this investigation is based on:

- Community Informatics.
- CRITICAL MASS
- FOAK (First of a kind in 30 centric approach).
- INNOVATION is the need of the hour.
- FORGET Short minded /Term Return.
- Reward doers not makers.
- Perception should not overrule reality.

"Survival of the fittest" and not "the survival of the strongest" is the growth theory of nature. That is why over the generations the cockroaches exist but dinosaurs have been extinct. In the information age the growth theory of the survival of the fittest is based on four mantras:

- Improved human resources to lead.
- Global information on desk to guide.
- Innovate to flourish.
- Quality to nourish.

Noble Laureate of Chemistry, Ilya Prigogine once said, "We can't predict the future, but we can prepare it." Certainly the future will be what we make of it with today's singlemost technology, IT. The success and the effectiveness of the changes will be measured with proper perspectives in future. But it has undoubtedly brought an unprecedented change in education and learning by giving time, space and volume continuity. Today education and learning like business and commerce have no geographic boundary, no volume restriction, and no time limitation. They provide just-in-time and just-on-scale solutions. On the scale of effectiveness, the business is measured by the low of the loss (W) of process cost. If P is the process cost, OPE (Overall Process Efficiency) is the efficiency factor of business, $W = P - (P \times OPE)$. With application of IT, OPE increases causing W to fall. Besides, IT gives the competitive advantages to the business activities. Information technology believes that: **Investment + Web technology + Users = Big Profits**. In such a scenario, let us accept whole heartedly e-learning as "supplementing" learning process without thinking of throwing out books, teachers, and existing universities/institutes/schools. Let us incorporate e-learning in our changes due to IT adoption to make ourselves ahead in the race of making India-2010 vision a real reality and not a reality in pen and papers.

Last but not least, we take lesson not only from teachers but from our parents (particularly mother) also. Mother is our first teacher. She first teaches us "how to walk", "how to eat" "how to call", and in fact "how to live with and grow." Therefore, I am a stunt believer that until and unless my

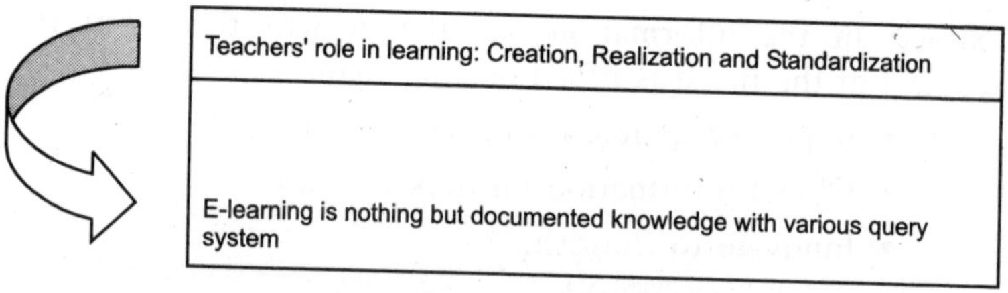

Fig. 4.2: E-learning exists at the mercy of teachers only

friends those who believe future will throw out books, teachers and universities/institutes/schools for making wholesale paths for e-learning, devise any technology for electronic mother, their attempt to enforce e-learning replacing all teachers from our society will be an exercise in complete futility. This is my e-learning (surely not electronic but experienced learning).

4.5 SOLUTIONS FOR IMBALANCES

True, the private initiatives have outscored (Fig. 4.5)[13] the government initiatives in higher education but the avenue so opened remains confined in degree and postgraduate level engineering and management education, and in a very limited way in medical education. Again then, the private initiatives in engineering education at present is mainly restricted to the market oriented courses (Fig. 4.5) of Computer Science and Engineering, Electronics Engineering, and Information

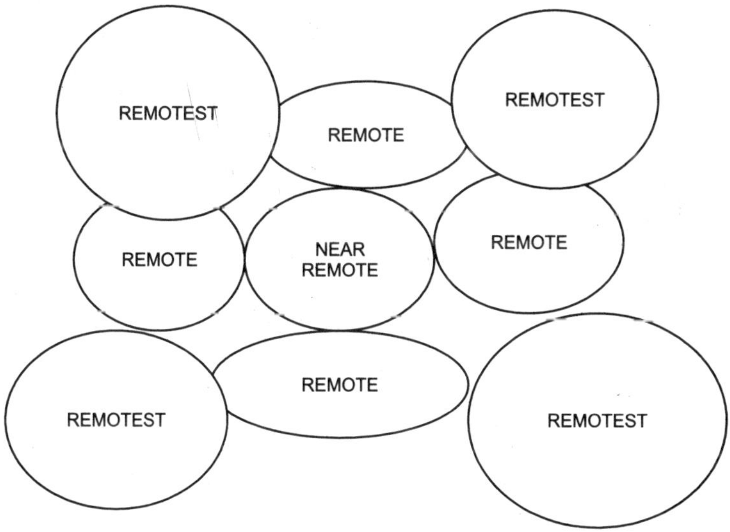

Fig. 4.3: Selection of changes

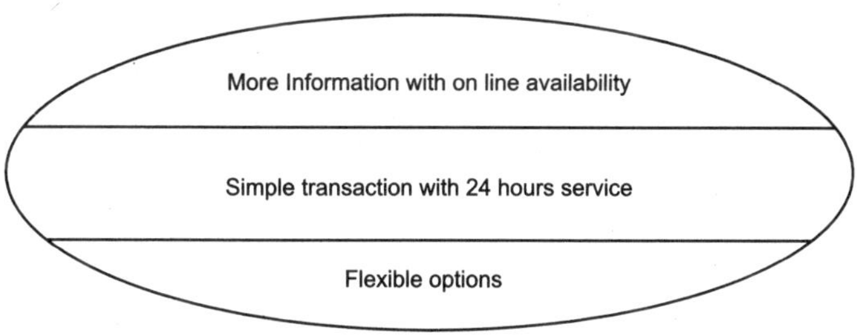

Fig. 4.4: Factors of e-learning

Technology. Ill attention has been noticed in the disciplines like Civil, Chemical and Mechanical engineering that are actually mother engineering. The basic disciplines of science in higher education like physics, chemistry, mathematics, philosophy and economics, etc. are not offered in the private institutes and universities. This will create an imbalance in the higher education system and the imbalance so created will have adverse effect in future both in terms of availability of scientists and engineers at proportional level and in related expertise and development. A plan and regulation from the regularity authorities of Ministry of Human Resources

Development and All India Council for Technical Education is the need of the hour to stop further widening of the imbalance. The regulation may be of the form of approving the private institute only when the institute agrees to run at least a mother engineering course per each three or less market demand courses, and one master program in the basic science per each five market driven courses.

The availability of good directors/senior teachers (particularly at the level of professors), in general, in private institutes has become a difficult task. The attraction of secured permanent and higher status job of government institutes/universities is one of the reasons behind this, although another reasonable attraction is that the government servants are usually preferred for prestigious position of brand institutes/universities at the level of Director/Vice Chancellor. Equally competent and qualified professors in the private institutes/Universities are often ignored. This further, is sometimes compounded when the authority of private institutes/universities do prefer professors of government institutes/universities for such positions in their institutes/universities. In general the teachers in the government institutes/universities are more qualified and competent, but there are teachers in private sectors also who are in no way inferior to the teachers of the government establishment. To make for the imbalance of the availability of good Directors/ Vice Chancellors and teachers between government and private institutes/universities, the teachers must be looked beyond his affiliation but on his teaching, research and administrative competency and ability. A plan of action in that direction is absent now, and for proper and equal opportunity to the private initiatives it has become imperative to begin with a plan. It would not be unsound if the proposal for the grading of Professors of all institutes approved by MHRD/AICTE is introduced purely on the basis of the achievement and points so earned. This may be done in line with accreditation of institutes currently being done for the institutes/universities. For grading of professors at different level purely based on points a reference table is suggested (Table 4.2).

The present imbalance among the graduate level engineers, post-graduate level engineers and doctorate level engineers is alarming due to sudden huge increase in intake capacity of degree offered by increasing number of private colleges. The problem has further compounded due to the fact that in post-graduate level engineering education, on average 21% sanctioned seats remain vacant and then 31% is the drop out. The decline trend in Ph.D. in engineering is shown in Fig. (4.7). The major reason for this is that the students take the postgraduate studies and the Ph.D. as stopgap arrangement before getting suitable job. Neither the postgraduate education nor the Ph.D. has been seriously thought of higher education in leading to meaningful research and development. Sometimes Ph.D. has been taken in general as a means for teaching jobs in the institutes/universities and for promotional purposes, rather than as a aim to become future international researcher/ scientist for the development of the subject and the technology. The solution needs a thorough review of degree and postgraduate level education in engineering. Today the subjects are becoming more and more interdependent and interdisciplinary in nature. An engineer of any branch today, needs to have knowledge and skill in three more interdependent subjects, namely environmental engineering, computer and electronics and communication engineering including Internet access besides other common subjects of communicative languages, cost analysis (economics), management, basic electronics engineering, electrical engineering, engineering physics, engineering chemistry, mathematics, workshop and drawing. There is an idea to change the admission procedure for engineering education in the changed scenario. The students may be admitted with no branch. After two years of common studies, based on grade points earned and choice, the discipline may be allotted. This will give a better opportunity for studying the basic subjects with vigor and seriousness that is mutely lacking amongst the students admitted on disciplinewise based on the score of entrance test. Similarly, there is a thought to revise engineering education in the form of integrated 5 years M.Tech. course after 10+2. Those who want to opt out with a job after 4 years study may do so, but they will be entitled to get B.Tech. degree after completion of project on job. The proposals need debate at the appropriate fora.

Conclusion

We have reviewed the scenario of the higher technical education in India in particular and in the developing countries in general in view of private initiatives and GATT agreement. It is noted with concern that facts and figurewise the problems and imbalances has resulted in the changed scenario. Attempts have been made in this paper to suggest a few remedial solutions for the existing problems keeping in mind the strategic need of more and better technical manpower generation for the developing countries[14-19] to meet the global challenges in the age of LPG (Liberalization, Privatization and Globalization). The concept of ICI has been moving long back as a cost effective and efficient approach for implementing state sponsored technical higher education. The NERIST project may be converted into an ICI for which several attempts were made but is yet to materialize. Other solutions for making private institutes to offer B.Tech. programme in mother engineering, post graduate courses and basic science courses may not face difficulty for implementing if vision and mission often noted by the private agencies in their applications made for approval to AICTE are accepted. The proposal for introduction of the national gradation of professors may be debated over different academic for a final acceptance.

Table 4.2: Points Proposal

(A) Educational Qualifications: Full Points= 25

Items on educational qualifications	Full point	Division of points based on grade of Universities/Institutes offering the degrees			
		***** University	**** University	*** University	** and Unaccredited Universities
D. Sc/ D. Engg.	5	5	4	3	2
Ph. D.		5	5	4	3 2
M.Tech. With 75% marks	5	5	4	3	2
With less than 75% marks	3	3	2	1	1
B.Tech. as in M.Tech.					
10+2	5	5 for first class	3 for class second	1 for pass grade	

(Contd...)

(B) Research and Development: Full Marks = 25

Items	Full points	Remarks
Per five or more publications referred journals in the last ten years	5	For less than 5 points will be proportional
Per twenty or more articles in reputed magazines in the last ten years	5	For less than 20 points earned will be proportional
Per 20 or more papers in national / International seminars/conferences, etc. in last ten years	5	-do-
Per 2 or more books authored and published in the respective field in last ten years	5	For less than 2 books it will be proportional
Per 2 or more sponsored research projects in the last 5 years	5	-do-

(C) Experience: Full Marks = 25

Items	Full points	Remarks
For 5 years or more as full professor Point be earned:-	5	For less than 5 years it is proportional
For 5 years or more as HOD	5	-do-
For 5 years or more as Dean	5	-do-
For 5 years or more as Director / Deputy Director/ Pro V C / V C	5	-do-
For member of national level board for 5 years or more	5	-do-

(D) Others: Full Marks = 25

Items	Full points	Remarks
Getting award of national / international level	5	One or more but one is the ceiling
Chairing 5 or more technical session at the international level conference outside India	5	For less than 5 it is proportional
Editors of referred technical journals for 5 years or more	5	-do-
Working in foreign lab on Fellowship for a period of 5 years or more	5	-do-

(*Contd...*)

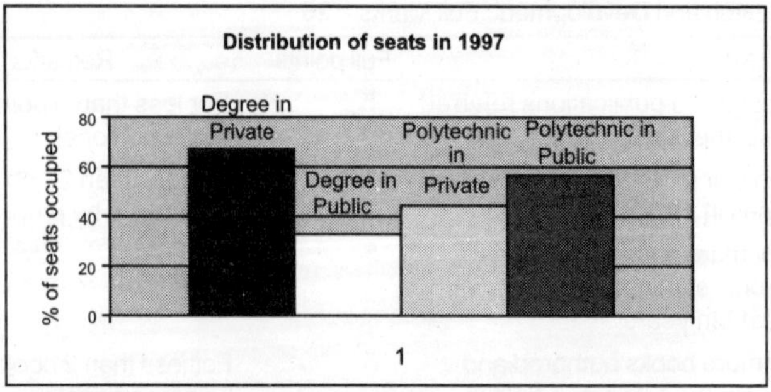

Fig. 4.5: Distribution of seats on different categories of institutes

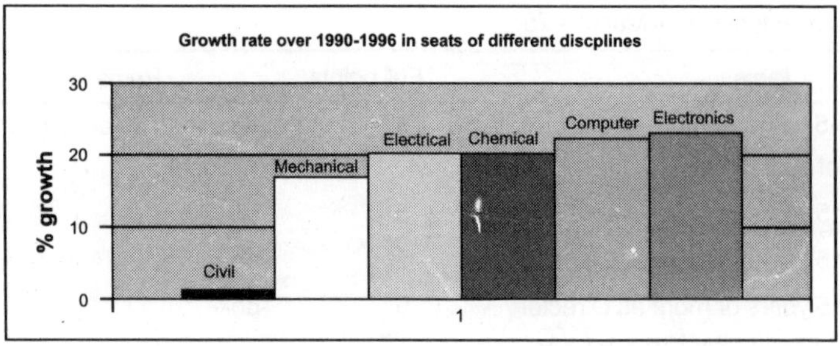

Fig. 4.6: Growth of different categories of institutes

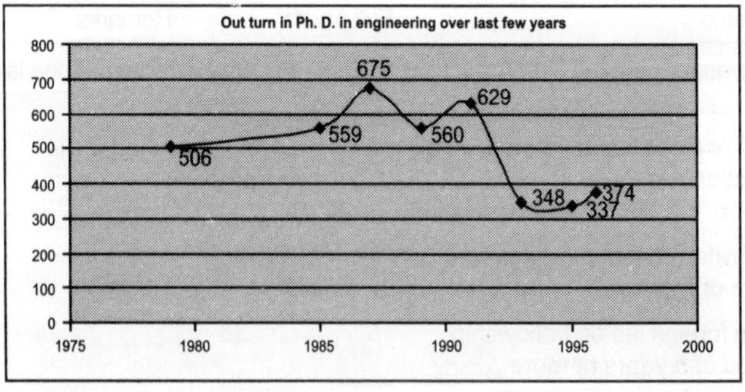

Fig. 4.7: Ph.D. statistics

Items	Full points	Remarks
Conduction summer / winter schools for 5 times or conducting seminar, etc. of national / international level 5 times / Fellowship of IEEE for 5 years	5	For less than 5 it is proportional

Notes

1. C.T. Bhunia, "People's Information System An Idea and Implementation", *CSI Communication,* Oct. 1992.
2. C.T. Bhunia, "Impact of Computer on Society and Technology", *Arunachal Pradesh Times*, April 1991.
3. A. James, F. Stoner et al., *Management*, PHI.
4. B.B. Bhattacharya and C.T. Bhunia, "Threats and Opportunities in the Higher Education in the Context of GATT", Communicated to *University News*, 2003.
5. C.T. Bhunia, "Overcoming High Cost of Higher Education, *University News*, June 2003, pp. 6-12.
6. C.T. Bhunia, "Hybrid Approaches in Higher Education", *National Seminar on Manpower Development and Utilization*, NIT, Rourkela, 2004, p. 5.
7. C.T. Bhunia, "Institute-cum-Industry", *University News*, Aug. 1994, pp. 11-14.
8. C.T. Bhunia et al., "A Model Structure of ICI of Electronics and Computer Engineering", *Proc ISTE National Seminar Cum Workshop on Management of Technical Education*, Bhopal, 1995, pp. 1-7.
9. C.T. Bhunia et al., "ICI revisited", *University News*, Nov. 1995, pp. 1-4.
10. C.T. Bhunia, "Person Power Development – Why and How", *CSI Communication*, Feb. 1997.
11. C.T. Bhunia et al., "Technical Education and Training for the Information Age", *Productivity,* Vol. 39, No. 4, pp. 579-587.
12. C.T. Bhunia, "Institute-Cum-Industry Revisited", *University News,* Association of Indian Universities, Nov. 1995, New Delhi, pp. 1-4.
13. Nancy DiTemase et al. (1994), "Degrees and Diversity at Work", *IEEE Spectrum,* USA, 1994, pp. 38-40.
14. S. Basu (1995), "Education for 21st Century", *University News,* Nov. 1995, pp. 5-6.
15. Edward Said (1999). "Academic Freedom Involves Risk and Danger", *The Asian Age*, 19 July, p. 12.
16. C.T. Bhunia, "People's Information System An Idea and Implementation", *CSI Communication,* Oct. 1992.

17. C.T. Bhunia, "Impact of Computer on Society and Technology", *Arunachal Pradesh Times*, April 1991.
18. A. James, F. Stoner *et al.*, *Management*, PHI.
19. Robert G. Murdick, "MIS Development Procedures", *Journal of System Management*, December 1970.

References

AICTE BOOK, 1998.

Bill Ratterec, "The prospects for teachers", *UNESCO Courier*, April, 1996, p. 26.

C.T. Bhunia et al. (1999), "Technical Education and Training for the Information Age", *Productivity*, Vol. 39, No. 4, pp. 579-587.

C.T. Bhunia (1994), "Institute cum Industry – A New Model for Technical Education", *University News*, Aug. 29, pp. 11-14.

C.T. Bhunia (1996), "Person Power Development – Why and How", *CSI Communication*, pp. 7-11.

C.T. Bhunia et al. (1995), "A Model Structure of ICI of Electronics and Computer Engineering", *Proc ISTE National Seminar*, Feb. 14-15, pp. 1-11.

C.T. Bhunia, "Higher Education Restructuring and Productivity", *University News*, Association of Indian Universities, Jan. 3, 2000, New Delhi, pp. 1-4.

Constantine N. Anagnostopolous & Lauren A. Williams (1998), "Few Gold Stars for Pre-college Education", *IEEE Spectrum,* April, pp. 18-26.

Edward Said, "Academic freedom Involves Risk and Danger", *The Asian Age*, 19 July, 1999, p.12.

Gerardo R. Ungson & John D. Trudel , "The Emerging Knowledge-Based Economy", *IEEE Spectrum*, May, 1999, pp. 60-65.

James B. Cowie, "Entering the Information Age", *IEEE Tech and Society*, Dec. 1989.

K.R. Shanmugam et al. (1998), "Returns to Higher Education: Estimating Using A Flexible Functional Form", *Productivity*, Vol. 39, No. 1, pp. 97-101.

Lane Wagger, "Transcendectal Meditation", *Indian Management*, March 1997.

Nancy DiTemase et al., Degrees and Diversity at Work, *IEEE Spectrum*, 1994, pp. 38-40.

S. Basu, "Education for 21st Century", *University News*, Nov. 1995, pp. 5-6.

Stephen Hawking (1995), "Life in the Universe".

The Telegraph (1999), *HDR Report*, 13 July, p. 15.

Tibor Braun, Wolfgang Glanzel and Andras Schubert (1999), "A Global Snapshot of Scientific Trends", *UNESCO Courier*, May, pp. 28-29.

Yashwant Deva (1998), *IETE Newsletter*, March–May, p. 10.

Yaswant Deva, "Information Infrastructure", *JIETE Tech Review,* Nov.-Dec. 1996.

Different Issues of Private Technical Education

5

5.1 IN GATT SCENARIO

Under the GATT (General Agreement on Trade in Services), the education has been defined as a lucrative commodity. It has fallen under an international trade category meaning any one can trade anywhere with education as a "thing". In addition, due to adoption of the liberalized economy and the consequent WTO and World Bank efforts the developing nations are restricted to invest in higher education. But on the other hand several researches and studies conclusively established the improved human resources generation as the sound strategy for competitive advantages in the open economy. A report of a task force of UNESCO said: "Without improved human capital, countries will inevitably fall behind and experience intellectual and economic marginalization and isolation.... In the developed world education is a major political priority." Another study over 58 countries suggests that the returns of higher education in per cent are 13, 13 and 16 respectively in Sub-Saharan Africa, Asia and Latin America and the Caribbean. Two immediate consequences of GATT adoption of education are: Privatization of higher education and international trading with higher education. The international trade of higher education till date is mainly carried out by the private institutes/universities rather than government institutes/universities.

The investment in higher education establishment is high. Due to financial crunch and restrictions under GATT agreement, the developing countries cannot afford high investment on higher education, natural consequence of which is the private investment and participation in higher education that makes the higher education a real commodity and commercial venture. This has several opportunities as well as threats that need careful analysis and consideration for future planning.

Opportunities

India ranked 141 out of 173 countries in the overall education index in the year 2000. In Human Development Index in 2001, India ranks 127 out of 175 countries with China and Victnam respectively at 104 and 109 position. India ranks below even most developing countries in terms of enrolment per 1,00,000 inhabitants. Out of several other parameters behind such a poor position, one was the non-availability of higher education institutes. With private participation, the opportunities for higher studies increases, and this may increase the enrolment figure comparable to other developing countries. This is supplemented by a statistics of West Bengal. Before addition of about 45 private engineering colleges in West Bengal in recent years, out of about 1,00,000 students appearing for the joint entrance examination only about 5,500 could make it. After establishment of Jalpaiguri Government Engineering College in 1968, the West Bengal Government took around 27 years to open another Government engineering college in Kalyani in 1995.

Several educational commissions including Kothari Commission argued for active industry and institute interaction for effective research and development. The private institutes sponsored by the industry houses can more efficiently and meaningfully realize the industry institute interaction for fruitful achievements. At the same time, the resource crunch for R & D activities may be overcome by the industry sponsored institutes.

Although debatable it is often said that private sectors are more disciplined and efficient than the government sectors. This being a case, it is expected that the education will be more efficiently and in a more disciplined way be imparted in the private institutes.

It is undoubtedly that a corporate culture will prevail in the private institutes that are absent in public institutes.

Due to financial crunch, the students of the developing countries could not study at the universities of the developed countries. But due to GATT, the universities of the developed countries are opening branches at the developing countries that will provide a scope to the students of the developing countries to study at the universities of the developed countries at a relatively low cost.

Threats

Adam Smith said, "It is not from the benevolence of the butcher ... or the baker that we expect our dinner, but from their regard to their own interest." Here lie all theories of investment by private sectors. Profit or in gentle word return on investment as often told in the education sectors, is the ultimate motive. The profit motive has natural attraction for quality degradation. Low teacher-student ratio of the existing private institutes in general has this reflection. However, profit being only motive is dangerous and counter-productive in education sectors.

As a consequence of ever-increasing marketization of higher education due to GATT, the basic disciplines like physics, chemistry, mathematics, languages, philosophy, history and geography, etc. are not offered in the private institutes and universities. The private investment still is oriented to courses of market demand. This will create an imbalance in the higher education system. In India most of the private engineering colleges offer courses in Computer, Electronics and IT and hardly any mother engineering like mechanical, electrical, civil, etc. The imbalance so created will have adverse effect in future both in terms of availability of engineers at proportional level and in related expertise and development.

The high tuition fees of higher education in private sectors will encourage only affordable societies to opt for. The meritorious poor students will not benefit from higher education opportunities offered by the private institutes. Is not GATT creating a further gap between haves and have nots in higher education? Generating scope for higher education for affordable students at the costs of non-affordable but meritorious students is bound to cast poor figure on quality on outputs and cause poor productivity.

A report of UNESCO in 2000 said, "...the private (for profit) sector has problems establishing quality programs that address anything other than short-term market driven needs."

Due to GATT adoption the international trade with higher education is a global issue. But the trade has amply become unidirectional i.e trade by developed countries in the developing countries. For example in Dhaka city of Bangladesh there are 42 centers of foreign universities but there is no such center of any Bangladesh university in any foreign country. This may make higher education trade like what software trade is today; and then all benefits of GATT inclusion of Higher Education will go to the developed nations.

Any higher education must have relevance to local needs. Besides, the local culture and national ethics and sentiment must be reflected in the higher education. With higher education by foreign universities, how far these can be achieved remains a mute question. It will be pertaining to mention here what Tagore said, "What I object to is the artificial arrangement by which foreign education tends to occupy all the space of our national mind and thus kills or hampers the great opportunity for the creation of a new thought power by a new combination of truths. It is this which makes me urge that all the elements in our own culture have to be strengthened...."

Overall the social appeal of the higher education must be belied with GATT adoption of the higher education. This is a big threat.

Due to adoption of open economy and GATT agreement and consequently the world bodies restrictions particularly on the developing nations for reduced budget for the higher education, a quite disturbing thing of appointing teachers on contract basis has cropped up that is bound to affect the quality of higher education and research that requires concentrated motivation and dedication.

Conclusion

The world declaration adopted by the 128 countries in 1998 at a conference on higher education of UNESCO noted: "The second half of this century will go down in the history of higher education as the period of its most spectacular expansion, an over six fold increase in student enrolments world wide, from 13 million in 1960 and 82 million in 1995. Without adequate higher education and research institutions providing a critical mass of skilled and educated people, no country can ensure genuine endogenous and sustainable development and, in particular, developing countries and least developed countries cannot reduce the gap separating them from the industrially developed ones." Therefore in line with GATT, the private institutes are to stay till government is in a position to adequate investment in higher education sectors; but with government controls and monitoring so that quality is maintained and any sort of undesirable imbalance is prevented for which it will not be wrong on the part of AICTE if AICTE imposes that the private institute be approved if they offer at least one mother engineering course and offer at least 5% tuition free seats to poor but meritorious students. For permitting foreign universities to operate, the monitoring of course curriculum with national ethics and philosophy and condition for equal opportunities in their countries be imposed only not to make the trade unidirectional as in software business.

5.2 CAN HYBRID APPROACHES IN HIGHER EDUCATION BE A SOLUTION?

"Without improved human capital, countries will inevitably fall behind and experience intellectual and economic marginalisation and isolation .... In the developed world, education is a major political priority." — UNESCO. Education at all levels is imperative for all-round development of any nation and it has become more and more important in the present age of competitive globalised economy guided by emerging technologies. Education being the basic and main backbone of a nation undoubtedly is a component of social infrastructure that the government must liberally invest in, besides controlling and monitoring as well as raising the quality of education. The improved human resource generation has been tested over history and proved beyond doubt, as the sound strategy for competitive advantage, yet the poor and developing nations under compulsion and resource crunch fail to fully implement the strategy. The developing countries in general face acute problem of funding the high cost of higher education. It has several dimensions:

- Due to high cost of higher education, although high cost involved in higher education is a debatable issue on several aspects, the developing countries fail to increase the number of higher educational institutes causing percentage of availability of higher education per person decreasing.
- The stated decrease in percentage as above is compounded multifold due to high increase in enrolment ratio with growing population. The enrolment in tertiary education in India in 1970, 1985 and 1995 were respectively 4.9%, 6.0% and 6.5%. India ranked 141 out of 173 countries in the overall education index in the year 2000. India ranks below even most developing countries in terms of enrolment per 1,00,000 inhabitants.
- The imposition of globalized economy has several restrictions on investment on higher education forcing the developing and poor countries to further fall behind in higher education scenario. At the same time given the current scenario, no government is able to pull out of globalization.
- It is an irony that the developing countries in order to compete with the developed nations, blindly try to copy or follow the higher education system/structure of the developed nations. The natural consequences happen in the form of wide mismatch between the requirement, supply and demand, one component of which is seen in the brain drain or reluctant brain drain. This causes the return on investment to decrease that acts heavily behind the investment by government.

- It is most unfortunate that the pattern of investment in the higher educational institutes/universities lack merits causing many great universities/institutes not getting grants as appropriate or productive based, whereas other low productive based universities/institutes getting higher share of budget. This causes the negative avalanche in the productive growth of the higher education.
- Due to GATT adoption the next natural step of globalization, the private initiatives in higher education has been noticed in the developing countries. But several studies have clearly demonstrated the huge imbalance in the process that may be counter-productive.

After India's participation in LPG (Liberalization, Privatization and Globalization) and after GATT adoption, the private initiatives in the higher education in India (and in general in developing countries) have increased in manyfolds. But honestly speaking the initiatives lack directions. The several imbalances and unequal growth of higher education due to unplanned growth of private higher educational institutes may cause severe damage to the very fabric of higher education without repair. In Figs. (1 & 2), we have shown just two major imbalances caused by private participation in higher education in India. In one developing country, our neighbors, the picture is gloomier. The issues were factually and exhaustively studied and a few unique solutions were suggested previously. The simple derivation of inevitableness of coming up of private initiatives in higher education has several questions that remain unanswered. After all, private institutes are not philanthropic establishments, rather they are mostly profitable in nature. These institutes earn return-on-investment and profit by charging high tuition fee. Then why are the governments not establishing private-nature institutes that will be solely run on tuition fee? After all, governments may not want profit, in which case the tuition fee will be lower than that of private institute. The question of only initial investment is the issue. But is it not that the private institutes mostly use the public money, in the

form of bank loan, for initial investment? Why are the governments not doing the same way for initial investment? Is it due to lack of vision or understanding of the issue? It is ample clear that the failure of government institutes lies with management not with money. The issue is very clear: The government institutes lack proactive approach that is due to bureaucratic functioning. Added with this, the so secured government service often makes its employees to become un- or non-productive. Thus, **why not to go for a solution that will use best of two approaches:** namely financially state sponsored and state controlled and monitored but solely privately managed/ administered institutes. Let private committee frames, operate and run the institutes.

5.3 DUAL OR CONTRADICTORY POLICIES IN THE GLOBALIZATION PROCESS

Dual Role

Over history, the best-known definition of a government is that the government is for the people, by the people and of the people. At the present context how far the Indian government is by the people and of the people is debatable. A sizeable section of people think, Indian governments, both state and central, are by and of the political parties. Individual or self-democracy has been lost to party democracy. Even then, a government could be a worthy if it is for the people. Since 1992 India has taken part in the liberalization, privatization and globalization process.

Long back many small and poor countries took part in privatization and globalization processes, put forward by the developed countries as an instrument of development. There are both success and failure stories of these countries. While Brazil is an example of great failure, South Korea is a great success. To get competitive advantages in the era of open economy, strong national infrastructure development is essential. A national infrastructure has two components: physical and social. Transport, power and telecommunication are the important physical infrastructures. Social infrastructures are education, health, sanitation, etc. Prof. Amartya Sen, first Asian who won Nobel prize in economics, comparing the privatization process of the Brazil and that of the South Korea held the Brazil's failure of development of social infrastructure as the basic reason for its failure in privatization and liberalization process. Any government sincerely desiring to be a leader in open economy should allow full private participation in development of physical infrastructure, and keep the social infrastructure under complete government control. Unfortunately, the policy and programme of present central government neither conform to this theory of successful participation in open economy nor reject it. The result is confusion, conflict and chaos among decisions, action and policies of the government.

Improved human resource generation, a social infrastructure has been accepted world over as a sound strategy for any development process. The national human resource generation depends on both the elementary education, and the higher education. Both are essential, and one should not be at the cost of other. The education, both the elementary and the higher, should be kept under complete government control. But the government is functioning otherwise. The reduction of higher education budget is a wrong decision and it should be counter-productive in near future. India's public expenditure on tertiary education, expressed, as a percentage of total public expenditure on education was 15.5% in 1985. The problem has further compounded due to population growth whose effect is the increase in gross enrolment ratio. This ratio expressed as a percentage of the population in tertiary education in India had jumped from 4.9% in 1970 to 6.5% in 1995. Again, it does not mean that generation of technical manpower is significant in India or in poor countries. In 1990, the total number of scientists and engineers per million population was 2807, 1665, 158, 3317 and 109 respectively in the developed countries, the Europe, the developing countries, USA and India. This reflects that poor countries including India need to generate more technical manpower by opening more and more technical colleges and universities. There is hardly any logic in the government's argument that higher education budget has been reduced to increase budget of the elementary education, as the higher education and the elementary education are no replacement of each other but two essential components for growth and development. Beside neither the argument that the higher education is so costly that the government cannot afford to, nor the proposition that return on investment is low has a sound basis for acceptance. Higher education is not costly in India compared to other countries. Higher education has been made costly because of wrong policies of government. Higher education does pay if return of higher education is made to use. Even in project specific matters, the final decision rests with bureaucrats rather than technocrats. Result is our prolonged dependence on imported technology and machines, although political parties when in power do not forget to claim that India is third technological manpower in world. Thanks to Mr. Pitroda, due to him India is at least not importing RAX (Rural Automatic Exchange — for rural telephone).

Government is inviting NRIs (Non-Resident Indians) to invest but forget that most of NRIs are product of higher education and return of investment of higher education in terms of NRIs investment is unparalleled to investment in any other sector. Government has reduced subsidy to higher education, placing higher education as non-merit service. If higher education is non-meritorious sector, there shall be nothing in the country to qualify for meritorious sector; likewise if defense budget goes on increase at the cost of developmental budget there shall be no country to defend.

The government has invited private initiatives in higher education. The irony is that private parties establishing higher educational institute are doing so for business and benefit and take it for granted that they are not for generous social works and responsibility. Private institutes are being built at the cost of parents and by means of higher tuition fees or by back door donations. The problem of government to establish institutes in the path of private parties is not known. Government institutions established in private parties' way are believed to be better than private institutes. Government may rethink of going private ways in higher education.

The existing policy of government for students' fee structure needs immediate review, in light of India's socio-economic gap. India is neither U.S. nor U.K. There is very wide and multilevel economic gap among peoples of India. Keeping same fee structure for all students is irrelevant in India. Fee structure should be multilevel; each level being applicable to the financial ability of parents. Multilevel fee structure is effective as the poor but meritorious students can go for higher education at low cost and at the same time, the revenue of higher education will increase by higher fees of rich students.

While the government in the name of privatization and liberalization is reducing budget for higher education, advocating for downsizing manpower in government sectors, and announcing for privatization of STD (Subscribers' Trunk Dialing) (as announced by the Prime Minister in recent conference of IT ministers), at the same time the government is introducing free telephone to all employees of telecommunication department, continuing to offer free pass (higher class, of course) to railways employees and free air tickets to employees of Indian Airlines and Air India. It will be pertaining to mention here that employees of higher education are not enjoying free education and no admission-bar neither for their wards nor for them.

Under such a scenario, a state of confusion and chaos exists. Whether government is for true liberalization or for liberalization in selected sectors or for liberalization for all but government employees needs to be clarified by the government.

Are We in Favor of "Private Investment in Education" or "Private Education"?

The present state of privatization in India at least raises a question as above. If India does private investment in education, nothing wrong is in it. But if privatized education what to my mind in the name of private investment in education is being done, the SWOT analysis of chapter 4 may be referred to. That says for a control of quality. If the quality fails, the so far earned reputation of Indians degrees in the world market will be bound to degrade. This will be counter-productive. India needs to understand this simple thing very carefully and on time for proper measure.

Contradictory Policy

India has taken part in LPG. If LPG is for improvement and development, the application areas of LPG must be decided with sufficient thoughts and substantial research based analysis. It, in all probability, appears that India intended to open just business to privatization process and global market in other name of LPG. This is where conclusively the LPG process fails to yield any result for the common people. It is an established fact that the good government is a component of economic development. No economic developmental process will be a success without good administration to implement the process. The basic administrative fabric in India is a well-established fact of corruption. The prolonged exercise to employ people recruited through established government agencies in a cadre structure in governmental administration has not reduced corruption but has indeed increased it. Thus no government apparently has achieved any economic development as expected from their policies and schemes. The participation in LPG has a scope to bring the stoppage in cadre structure that is to my mind is a source of organized corruption. The LPG in fact is itself an open structure, and it does not believe in closed system. It is not understood why the successive government favoring LPG has not undertaken initiative or steps to implement LPG in cleaning government administration. If our successful ministers who are not from any cadre structure can efficiently and successfully run ministries, this itself is the conclusive evidence that non-cadre people are there to run administration efficiently. It is a well established fact in India that till today professors, writers and thinkers, Social workers, doctors and artists are less corrupt than the cadre officers. I wonder whether government can selectively employ them as District Magistrates, Police Chiefs and Secretaries and Commissioners to build new India as a leader of LPG. Any exercise for realizing "India Shining" or "Building India to Shine" must have this type of innovative but bold exercise for cleaning the government first or making the very fabric of the government administration to openness in the LPG process.

6 Maintaining Quality in Higher Education

6.1 HOW TO INSTILL QUALITY IN TECHNICAL EDUCATION: A PRACTICAL APPROACH (PAD)

"Survival of the fittest" – is the slogan of the present age of global competition and liberalized open economy. Four mantras for being and keeping fittest are:

- Improved Human Resources to lead.
- Global Information on Desk to guide.
- Innovate to Flourish.
- Quality to Nourish.

Assume a nation to be a car. To drive this car, first two mantras are respectively the driver and the fuel. Last two mantras are the directions for and of driving.

Today, technical persons with high and improved quality are therefore of paramount importance for any nation. Prof A. Bhattacharjee, an eminent former Professor of Jadavpur University and a former Director of IIT Kanpur, reportedly made an observation that "IITs produce export quality engineers." But how? Keeping aside the fact that most brilliant students take admission in IITs, the reason of producing export quality manpower by IITs is 3 Bs of IITs:

- Better faculty members.
- Better physical infrastructure (laboratories, teaching aids and libraries).
- Better funding.

Thus, it is a mere logical extension that to instill quality in Technical Education, the most practical approach shall be to go for 3 Bs.

There is an earnet need for improving quality in Indian Higher Education. As of today we stand very poorly in world ranking of higher education (Appendix B).

6.2 ISSUES OF BETTER FACULTY MEMBERS

GO FOR PAD (Posting, Assessment and Duties and Discipline):

A. Posting, Recruitment, Promotion: Prof A. Dasgupta, a former professor of Management of the Delhi University, in a management conference opined that first step for improved human resources in any organization shall be "to go for recruiting people who are resources." For recruitment of faculty members we have to follow this benchmark theory of Prof. Dasgupta. Teachers are not available, so go for recruiting anyone and everyone as available, which is often the present practice, must be stopped. Recruitment by the present mode of selection, which often becomes election, must also be stopped. Recruitment by achievements shall have to be introduced. It is proposed that the recruitment and promotion and posting to the posts of HODs /Deans/Directors may be done purely on the basis of points earned by the achievements as one illustrated in Table (6.1). The UGC/AICTE, etc. may do grading of the Universities/Institutes and Journals. If required, by special perks and special pay, etc, the higher achievers shall have to be encouraged to join and continue as faculty members.

B. Assessment: The World Bank argued, "Higher academic performance can be promoted by evaluating the quality of teaching and research." Teachers' assessment is essential. Assessment by feedback from students is not a sound strategy. There is a difference between "sound Teacher and popular Teacher." For proper assessment, the examination of question papers set by the course teachers is being proposed. The review of the question papers shall address (i) whether the whole of the syllabus has been covered, (ii) what is the level of teaching, and (iii) whether there is any originality in teaching. Based on these, grades shall be awarded to the teachers, which shall further be recorded in ACR.

C. Duties and Discipline: To stop the deteriorating condition of the conduct, the discipline and the quality of the colleges and the universities, the University Grants Commission mooted the idea of introducing "a code of ethics for teachers, a code of conduct for staff and a code of discipline for students." Today we seriously need a code of not only ethics but also conduct and disciplines for the teachers. Today, in the educational institutes liberty is confused with license, thereby hardly any discipline and conduct are prevailing in the institutions. Vice Chancellors, Directors, Deans and Heads are often heckled and forced to resign or removed by the faculty members in the name of democratic rights. Even these are done often in collusion with the students and staff. These have being possible due to so-called rotational Deanship/Headship and contract appointment of Directors/Vice-Chancellors. If the rotational and contract appointment are so good, why is there no such scheme of rotational or contract appointment of the Chief Secretary/ Cabinet Secretary, etc? We need to seriously consider and rationalize the issue. It is strongly proposed that Heads/Deans and Directors be appointed on permanent basis and on the basis of grade points earned as per Table (6.1). With these, it is expected that discipline shall be restored among the faculty members.

There remains a confusion regarding duties and responsibilities of the teachers. Whether it is RAT (Research, Administration and Teaching), TAR or ART, etc., it is proposed that time has now reached to clearly define the duties at different levels and strictly adhere to it. The duties and the responsibilities may be defined as below:

Lectures/Sr. Lecturers: Teaching and Research and Laboratory set-up.

Asstt. Professors/Readers: Teaching, Research and Departmental Administration.

Professors/Sr. Professors: Institute Level and Departmental Administration, Research and Teaching.

6.3. ISSUES OF BETTER INFRASTRUCTURE AND FUNDING

Better infrastructure needs better funding. Both the issues can be tackled by converting the conventional educational institutes each into an ICI (Institute-Cum-Industry). State funding of higher education is becoming difficult day by day in poor countries like ours. ICI can solve the funding problems. In ICI, there shall be two sections: Institute and Industry. Industry section will earn money for the ICI. What is wrong if faculty members as they do consultancy work presently outside the institutes, can do the same in ICI? What is wrong if students do project work and laboratory work in the industry section of ICI in an environment of "learn while doing"? We badly need to change our educational structure from copied system of Western countries to our friendly system of ICI. ICI shall give a solid structure for quality education.

6.4 IS MORE NUMBER OF IITs ANY HOPE FOR INDIA

Reportedly, Dr. Murli Manohar Joshi as HRD Minister, announced for the setting up of another five Indian Institutes of Technologies (IITs). The declaration as and when will be implemented will certainly fulfill a long cherished dream of a large number of young bright aspirants who are hoping to get admission to IITs but are not able to get although they duly deserve it. This is due to the fact that the number of IITs were not increased keeping in pace with the population growth and hence the increased enrolment rate in higher technical education. This country although jumped in population from 40 crore during the independence age to 100 crore in 2000, has not established more than original five IITs till 1995 when understandably under a memorandum of understanding with the Assam Gana Parishad, the IIT of Guwahati was set up. In the recent past, the upgradation of the Roorkee University to IIT is just another addition. If five IITs were to suffice 40 crore of population of past, the country definitely deserves to have at least twelve IITs to serve the present population of 100 crores, although the current demand based on the trend of economy and technology is more. The enrolment in tertiary education in India in 1970, and 1995 were respectively 4.9% and 7.0% that is a clear indication of the enrolment growth with the increasing population. The need of IIT to take care of bright boys and girls in increasingly growing enrolment ratio is thus well understood and surely a long pending issue. There are several other dimensions in favor of the claim, one of which is the strategic long-term planning to effectively take part in the globalization process as a future leader rather than a follower.

It is a time tested and historically proved conclusion that the mastery over technology and the mobility with appropriately applied technology are what distinguish the north from the south or the developed from the developing. Thus the right model for the successful development for the developing countries is the generation of more and superior technical and scientific manpower in terms of knowledge, know-how, skill and innovative capability. The quantity and the quality improvement in human resources both are at the center of the need of the hour in India, and not just anyone of them only at the cost of the other. The importance of generating more technical manpower must not be diluted with our prolonged tall claim that we are the third largest technical manpower in the world, being next only to USA and the then USSR (or presently may be Russia). Such claim may have some realities in terms of absolute figures, but the actual merit requires figures on percentage population. Generating 10 gold coins out of 10 is highly powerful philosophy and resourceful strategy than generating 100 gold coins out of 1000. The scientists and engineers per million population in 1986 were 5,029, 3,317, 1,973, 1,287, 210 and 109 respectively in Japan, USA, France, Singapore, Thailand and India. India lags behind not only the developed countries but also the developing countries like Thailand. And exactly here the country needs the corrective strategy for worthy human resource reservoir. Any argument contradictory to this on the basis of other grounds like growing unemployment of engineers is unsustainable under several requirements and future possibilities. Besides, there remains a simple philosophy that the educated unemployed is in noway more harmful than the uneducated unemployed in the unemployment environment of a country but the educated unemployed youths contribute towards increasing the average education level of a country that is directly in proportion to the development of a nation. The developed countries have been experiencing unemployment since long back, yet they are not diminishing the education avenues because they have realized in letter and spirit that "without improved human capital, countries will inevitably fall behind and experience intellectual and economic marginalization and isolation." While generating more technical manpower, the nation needs to monitor and control any undue consequences resulted if any for the exercise. It will be pertaining to mention here the mushroom growth of private institutes in the exercise of creating more avenues for higher technical education thereby generating more technical manpower, has resulted in the imbalances in different forms in the higher education. True, the private initiatives have out- scored the government initiatives in higher education thereby opening the opportunities for generating more technical manpower but the avenue so opened remains confined in degree and postgraduate level engineering and management education, but no noticeable figures in medical education. Again then, the private initiatives in engineering education at present is mainly restricted to the market oriented courses of Computer Science and Engineering, Electronics Engineering, and Information Technology. Most ill attention has been noticed in the disciplines like Civil, Chemical and Mechanical engineering that are actually the mother engineering. The basic disciplines of science in higher education like physics, chemistry, mathematics, philosophy and economics, etc. are not offered in the private institutes and universities. This will create an imbalance in the higher education system and the imbalance so created will have adverse effect in future both in terms of availability of scientists and engineers at proportional level and in related expertise and development. While the role of the private initiatives in generating more technical manpower deserves due recognition, the imbalance created by their such exercise should not simply be overlooked in the greater interest of a nation if it has a plan of vision and mission to reach at the level of excellency.

In a recent article Ram Jethmalani clearly argued that in order to have effective utilization of the present world trade system, the poor countries' "main need and ultimate expectation from WTO" will be "free mobility of labor, skilled and unskilled." In a research on the individual's economic success, Professor Frank Leavy of Massachusettes Institute of Technology (MIT) showed that "education seems more closely tied than ever to an individual's economic success." Professor Laster Thurow of the same institute was quoted as saying "those with Third World skills will earn Third World wages." IITs in India play a crucial role in producing the 'export quality' human resources. The current space of information technology and the perceived knowledge technology of 21st century have opened a new opportunity and avenue for India that had a vast knowledge pool in ancient times. Management Guru Peter Drucker opined that, "the leading original group of the knowledge society shall be knowledge workers and knowledge executives who know how to allocate knowledge to productive use.... Unlike the employees under capitalism, they will own both the means of production and the tools of production... the crucial point about a post-industrial society is that knowledge and information become the strategic and transforming resources of the society, just as capital and labour have been the strategic and the transforming resources of the industrial society." Knowledge is becoming power and saleable; and the power is back to basics. Why not grab this situation? The Indian knowledge and intelligence base is world recognized that must seize the opportunity opened by the new and upcoming technologies to realize that India will regain the leadership in the world.

In setting up more IITs, two puzzles require proper readdress. Both the puzzles revolve around cost and cost-effectiveness. It is often said that return on investment in IITs is poor. The IITians leave the country and apply their expertise in development of other nations than that of their own country. This is called brain drain, but truly it is "reluctant brain drain." Had the right opportunities existed in India, the brain drain could have been limited if not nil. Due to brain drain, it is argued that the country does not get proper return on investment in IITs. But has the return in terms of NRIs (of IITians) investment in India been taken into this consideration? Truly the returns by means of investment of IITians of NRIs are unmatched for any other returns from related avenues. It is only a matter of chain actions and reactions that are needed for achieving more return on investment. Secondly, the establishment of an IIT involves huge investment. Can our country afford to the same whereas it needs to invest more in elementary and primary education and social infrastructure to take care of its more than 75% population living below poverty line? Really and logically the answer is a big 'NO'. Edouard Balladuar, former French Prime Minister in one of his articles, 'At the crossroads' wrote; "Everyone should have access to a general education, which is often the best way to acquire that range of diverse skills which enables people to adapt to future changes over the course of their lives. But our system of education should give more importance to technical and vocational training, and to make ties with business." Therefore, the alternative solution is the crying need, as the nation needs IITs too. The conversion of Roorke, University into an IIT in such a scenario is more than a right approach, and it is with this example of optimal solution, the government can set up IITs in no time. The country is not short of both central and state institutes that deserve to be IITs, and to name a few of them out of many such institutes/universities are Indian School of Mines, Jadavpur University, Bengal University of Engineering and Science (Bengal Engineering College, Shibpur) and Jawaharlal Nehru University.

6.5 ROLE OF AICTE IN QUALITY CONTROL

All India Council for Technical Education (AICTE) is the regulatory authority for technical education in India. The role of AICTE is restricted to approving establishment of institutes and courses. AICTE considers many parameters before according approvals and these major parameters include physical infrastructure, human resources, laboratories and libraries among many others. AICTE sends expert committee to evaluate these parameters and on the basis of the report submitted by the committee and the verification of supporting papers, the decision of approvals or otherwise is taken. Many times, objections about the visit of expert committee are raised. General objection refers to license raj system. The education needs quality assurance that is not guaranteed automatically in private venture because the private investment has a profit motive, neither it is guaranteed in government sectors where job is secured without any delivery. Thus AICTE visit has a positive role. The thing to be seen is that the objective of quality control is met by such visits. The AICTE report writing proforma for the year 2004-2005 is surely a failure in that direction. It requires modification in several respects. Any assessment must not be only restricted to checking the numbers and counts, but also see the productivity or how the availability is being used to meet the objective. Besides the numbers and counts must be quantitative rather than some descriptive. A proposed new proforma is suggested in line with the FILL factor discussed in previous section:

(i) For "F": Count number of faculty members considering and if and when (a) the faculty member meets minimum prescribed qualifications and experiences as prescribed by AICTE for that post, (b) the faculty member has got proper appointment offer, (c) the age of the faculty member is below the maximum limit prescribed by the respective government and pay is offered to the faculty member to his position as per AICTE norms. Based on the count, evaluation of the point earned may be made as guided in Table (6.1).

Table 6.1: Maximum 2 Points Scale

	Institute's availability	Point earned
Teacher: student ratio	1:x	(15/x) Note: [x=x when x=<15 and x=15 when x>15]
Professor: Assistant Professor: Lecturer	x1:x2:x3 ratio	0.33×{x1/(x2+x3)}×6 +0.33{x2/(x1+x3)}×(2/5) + 0.33 × {x3/(x1+x2)}×(3/4) where maximum point of each of the three components is limited to 0.33 only.

(ii) For "I": Evaluation may be made as shown in Table (6.2) again on a 2 points scale.

Table 6.2: Evaluation on 2 Points Scale

	Institute's availability	Points earned
PC: students ratio	1:s	(4/s) Note: s = s when s>=5, but s=4 else when s<5
Number of Internet Terminal: Students ratio	1:I	(8/I) Note I=I when I>=8 but I=8 else when I<8

(iii) For each of Library, Laboratory and other Infrastructure (land requirement/environment etc.), single step Table (6.3) may be used.

Table 6.3: On 2 Points Scale

	At what percentage meeting	Points earned
Quantity wise what percentage the institute meets with for AICTE requirement	P %	(P/100)
Quality wise what percentage the institute meets with for AICTE requirement	Q %	(Q/100)

FILL plus other infrastructure each on a 2 point scale with constitute a total of 10 points scale. The institute quality may now be assessed as in Table (6.4)

Table 6.4: Assessment of Institute Quality

Institute's earned point (EP)	Grade
EP≥8.5	Excellent
8.5>EP≥7	Very good
7>EP≥5.5	Good
5.5>EP≥4	Average
4>E P	Below average

6.6 QUALITY BY CONTROLLING INPUTS

Intakes in technical institutes and universities are made through joint entrance examination (JEE) at different states and national level with different variations in name of the examination. In recent times the sanity of these examinations are in doubt. Often the questions are leaked out before examination. A special issue of *University News,* a Journal of Association of Indian Universities, devoted on the subject was published on June 7-13, 2004. Two important issues of admission test based on JEE are:

(i) The students pay over attention (sometimes reluctantly but on pressure from parents) on admission related studies rather than on the subjects of class 10+2 courses. This is injustice to the national knowledge base. The poor knowledge of students in history, geography, philosophy, literatures and languages become stumbling blocks in making future generation of the nation to be good human citizens. It will be most pertaining to mention here the increased crime rate and the mental restlessness rate among others as shown in Fig. (6.1) with increased Internet penetration.

(ii) The students' growing apathy towards extra-curricular activities may be more counter-productive for honest and good future citizens. An engineer who writes poems and who sings is definitely better human than an engineer who does not do these and related other things.

For high quality intakes it is suggested that admission be made with criteria rather than just on single JEE:

Final Score for Admission (FSA) = 0.45 × % score in admission tests (It is proposed to take average score of two admission tests for consideration in order to tackle the questionable sanity of tests. For example: IIT admission, IIT may consider IIT JEE and WBJEE for students from West Bengal) + 0.45 × % score in board (10+2) test (with multiplication by possible national level normalization factor*) + 0.1 × % score in extra curriculum activities obtained in school.

*[say students of three boards A, B and C are applicants in any institute in a year and in that particular year highest % of marks scored are 99%, 89% and 90%. Then the normalization factor for the boards will be:

A = 1, B = 99/89, and C = 99/90 in general for a particular board the normalization factor will be (highest of all boards/ highest of a particular board]

6.7 CONCLUSION

We have proposed PAD and I-C-I respectively for operational and structural changes to instill quality education. FILL (Faculty, Internet, Library and Laboratory) is good, it is understood that quality will be good. It is an automatic system. PAD + FILL together constitute major quality maintenance and improvement instruments. For good human quality the suggested scheme for control of intakes may be thought of.

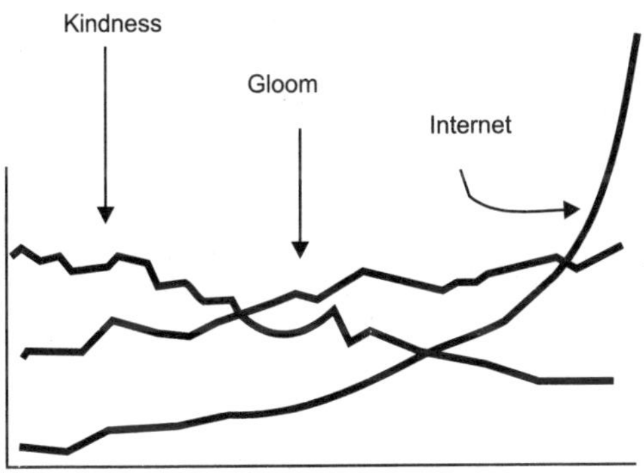

Fig. 6.1: Irresponsible internet statistics generator

7

Conclusion

The work gives a message to the Third World/developing countries. The message is portrayed below:

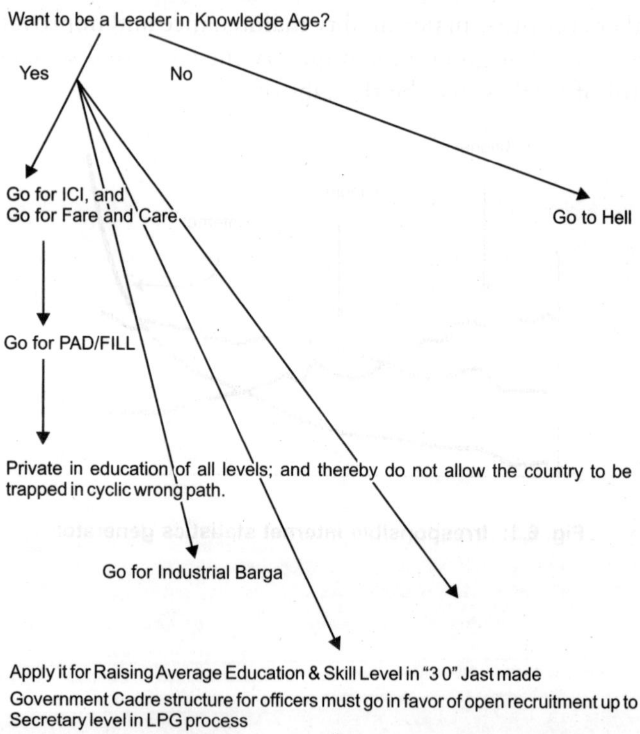

The world is believed to witness knowledge society in 21st century that has contrasting assumptions of people and technology from that of the 20th century as shown in Table (7.1). The proposals given in the current work duly conforms to the new assumptions of 21st century about people and technology.

Table 7.1: Comparison of Knowledge Society

About	20th century	21st century
People	Assumed as cost factor that must therefore be monitored and controlled	Assumed as assets that must be honored, valued and developed
Technology	Design technology to minimize human error and do work.	Integrated knowledge technology with social systems to enable knowledge based work.

It is very pleasing to note that the Jadavpur University has started to experiment on ICI type project. The university is in the process of taking over of National Instruments Limited, a sick industry for revival. More encouraging is the Oxford University's shift toward an ICI model. A report published in the *Asian Age* dated 17.4.2005 under the heading of "Oxford University to brand champagne" reads:

> Oxford University plans to cash in on its global academic brand. Except its prestigious degrees, the university hopes to offer a wide range of products bearing the Oxford stamp of approval in the open market. Scientific toys and games, Oxford branded champagne, garden tools and even baby clothes are to be sold to boost the university's income. Oxford Limited, a university subsidiary, has been set up with the stated aim of commercially exploiting "the knowledge, skills and crest of the University of Oxford."
>
> A little while ago commercial was in the same part of the Oxford English Dictionary as prostitution at this university", says Oxford Limited Managing Director Mike Davis said. Now the university is sending brand licensing packs to companies across the globe, inviting them to "exploit the quintessential British heritage of the university arms" through "aspirational life-style collections or product group categories."

Oxford trademarked its crest in 1993 and makes £ 400,000 a year from licensing its use. It hopes to increase that figure to about £ 5 million within five years. While American Ivy League universities offer office chairs, lamps and clocks, Oxford is taking a distinctly different approach. Mr. Davis said: "For US universities such as Harvard, a huge part of the business is high net value items. We're trying to avoid stuff like that. We want to sell things with a real relevance to Oxford; we want to romance the products with Oxford's heritage."

The university recently licensed toy manufacturer USI to produce the Oxford "Discover and Explore" young scientist range. Including crystal radios that are within the range of pocket-money earners, to costlier items such as microscopes and globes, with packaging bearing the names of famous Oxford scientists, the products will be in the shops in time for Christmas. London's exclusive Harrods store has accepted the entire series and negotiations are in progress to exploit the range nationwide.

John Hood, Oxford's Vice Chancellor, told the *Times*: "For over nine centuries the name Oxford University has been synonymous with excellence in teaching and learning. As guardians of this brand in the 21st century we have a duty to protect the name but equally we must consider ways to add value to the brand."

My theory of 1994 on ICI model is coming as a big way in UK but not in India. That is what is irony!

Appendices

APPENDIX A

Picture of Digital Divide World Over in Recent Years and its Variation with Different Parameters

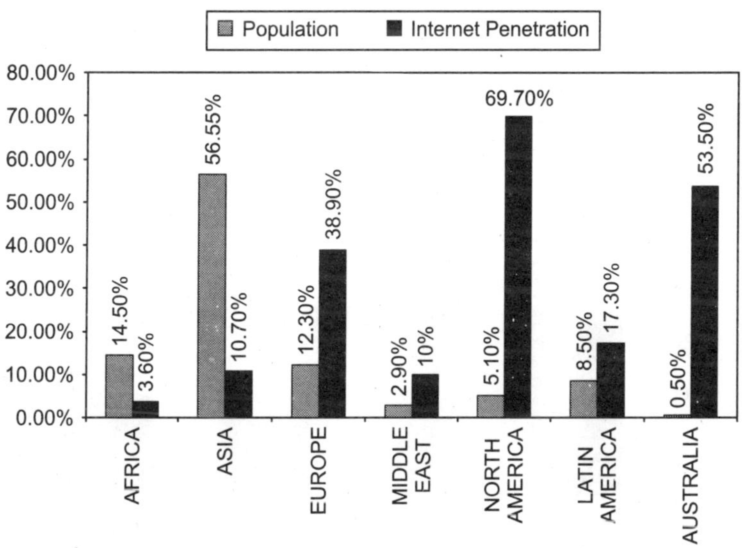

Fig. A1: Population and Internet Penetration with 1000 people in World Region in 2007

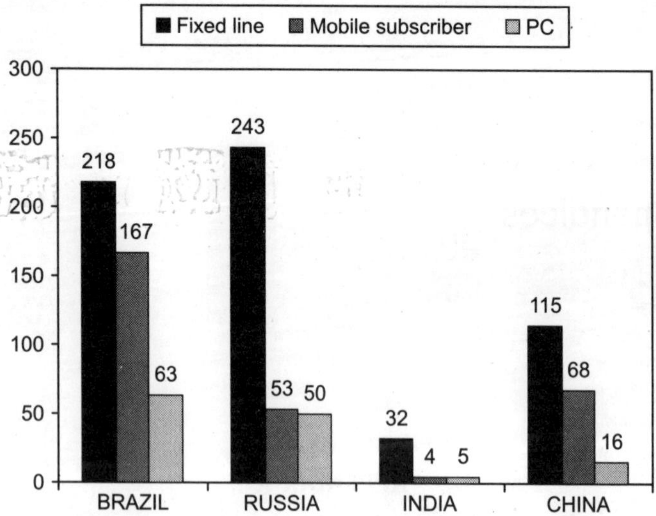

Fig. A2: IT Access within per 1000 people in BRIC in 2001

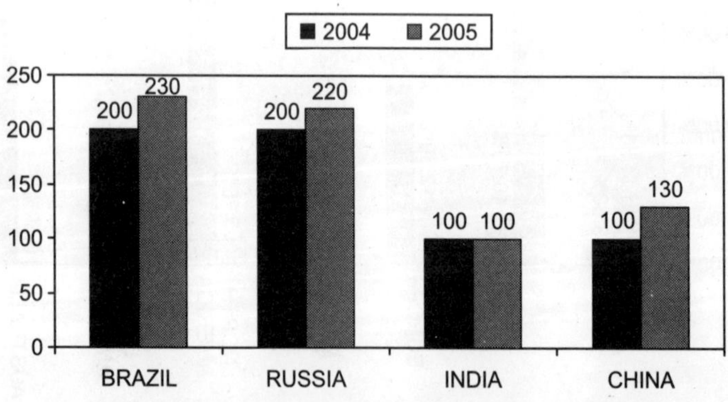

Fig. A3: Internet Penetration in BRIC in 2004 and 2005

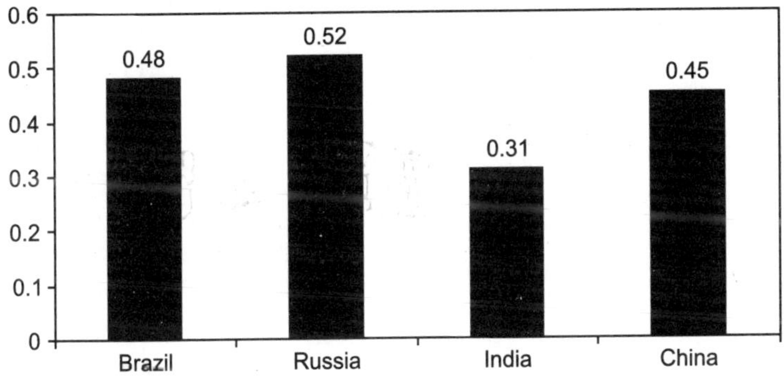

Fig. A4: Digital Opportunity Index in BRIC in 2005/2006

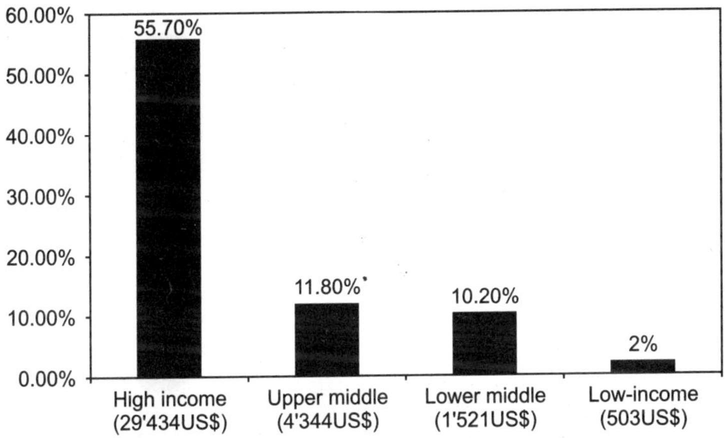

Fig. A5: Internet use in different income level in 2005

APPENDIX B — Ranking of Universities World Over

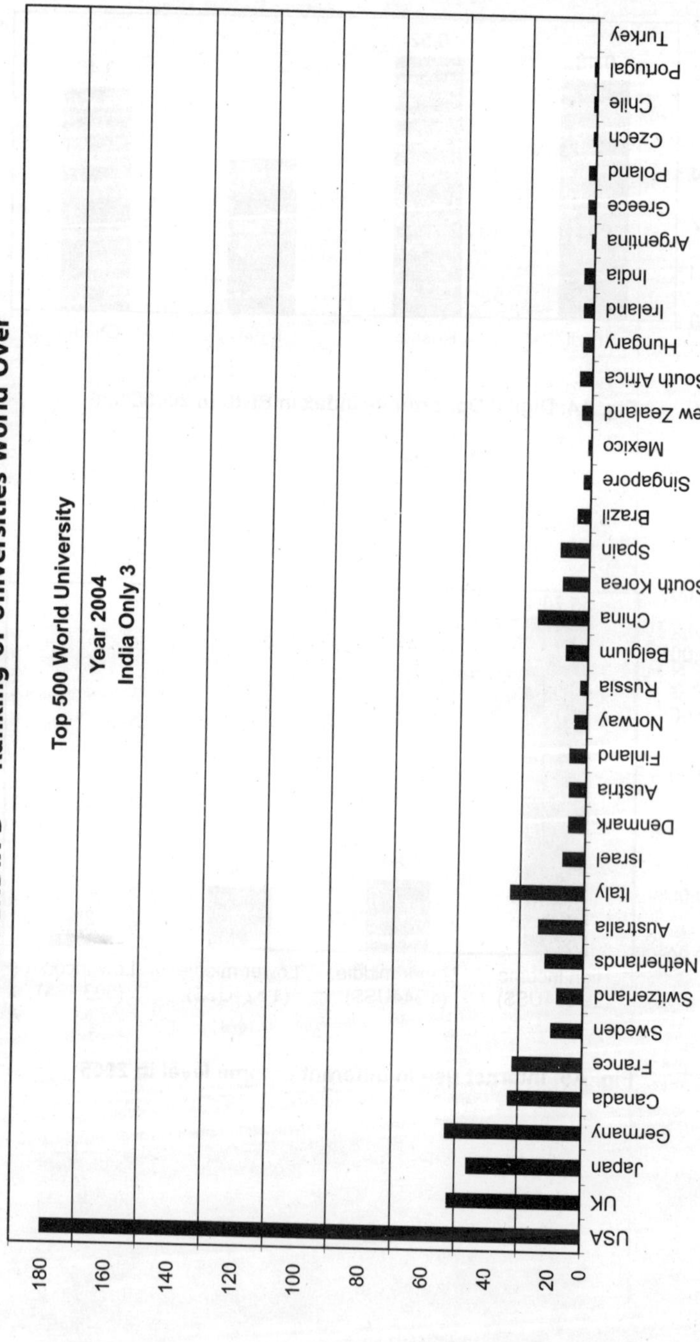

Fig. B1: Name of the Countries

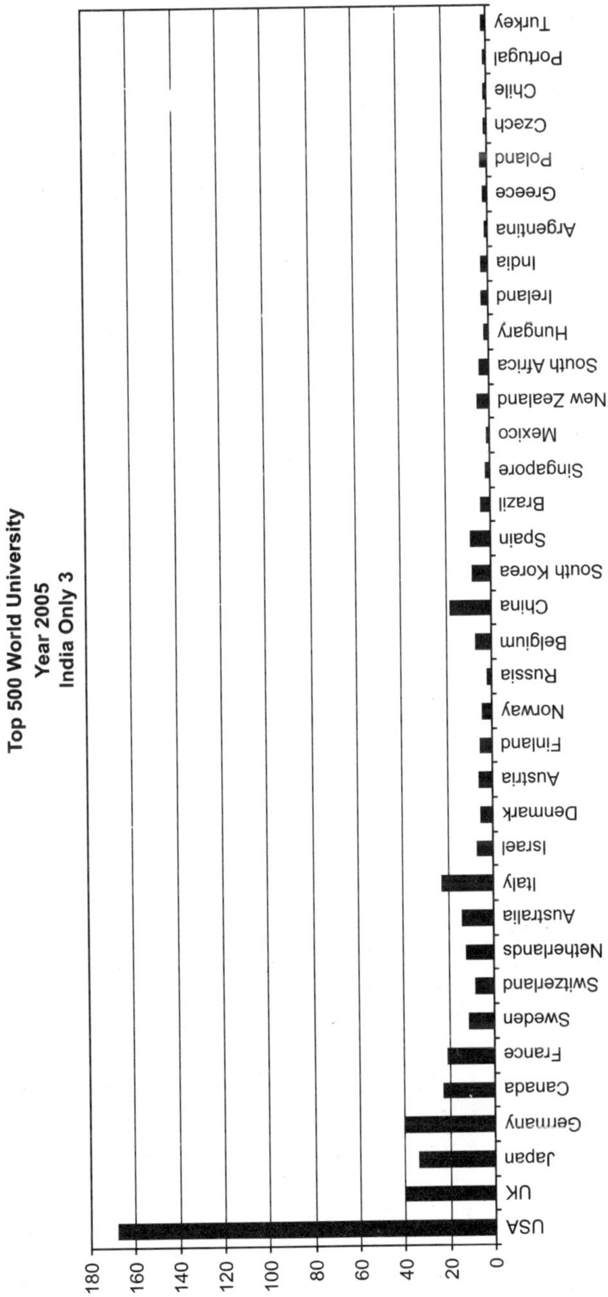

Fig. B2: Name of the Countries